What higher education professionals need

to know about *today's* students

CONNECTING TO THE
net.generation

NASPA
Student Affairs Administrators
in Higher Education

What higher education professionals need
to know about *today's* students

CONNECTING TO THE
net.generation

Reynol Junco &
Jeanna Mastrodicasa

FOREWORD BY
M. Lee Upcraft

NASPA
Student Affairs Administrators
in Higher Education

TABLE OF CONTENTS

Acknowledgments

I would like to thank the people who encouraged, supported, and helped me as I worked on this book. First and foremost, I thank my wife, Heather, and my son, Liam, the grounding forces in my life. Heather, you're an inspiration. Thanks for putting up with me while I stared at the computer for hours on end. I could never have done this without your love and support (and your willingness to get up at two-hour intervals throughout the night to take care of Liam). This book is for you. Let's hope we can understand where Liam is coming from as well as we've been able to learn about the Net Generation. Liam, you won't be able to read for a while, but I'll thank you anyway. Thanks, *bebito*, for putting a big smile on my face all the time. I'm looking forward to getting back into the late-night diaper change rotation.

I'm also grateful to Lee Upcraft, who came out of retirement to write the foreword to this book and has always supported me in my writing endeavors. Lee, thank you for giving me my first opportunity to be published in a book, and thank you for your mentoring, which has helped make me the writer I am today. I especially appreciate your ability to coax me into writing less like an automaton and more like someone with a pulse. Your perspective on student affairs not only reached into the recent past but helped me look into the future to consider what's on the horizon with our students.

A special thanks to Jeanna Mastrodicasa, the most pleasant person I've ever worked with, for putting up with my neuroticism throughout this process. I've been grateful for the complementary energies that have allowed us to push each other to think outside our personal comfort zones.

Jeanna and I could not have written the book without the help of colleagues and friends at institutions throughout the United State, as well as the NASPA national office staff. Thank you, Gwen Dungy, for your encouragement and for the opportunity to write this book. Thank you to Stephanie Gordon for your help with networking and to Melissa Dahne for your help with editing. Special thanks go to Ron Atwell at the University of Central Florida; Mary Ann Begley and Claire Wetterau at Bowling Green State University; Scott Harrison at Old Dominion University; Kandis Smith at the University of Missouri System; Glen Cope and M. K. Stallings at the University of Missouri-Saint Louis; Les Cook at Michigan Tech University; Linda Koch at Lock Haven University; and Dayanne Izmirian at the University of San Diego. Without your help, the Net Generation Survey would not exist. I'd also like to thank Chris Offutt at Lock Haven University for her suggestions on the Net Generation Survey and for quickly producing the paperwork I needed for other institutions' institutional review boards.

Last but not least, a special thanks to all the students who helped us along the way. Jeanna and I have learned much more about the Net Generation from our own students (whether they were intentionally teaching us or not) than we would ever have been able to glean through literature reviews and data analyses. Special thanks go to Melanie Shellhammer and Leigh Ann Miller for their exacting data cleaning skills. Thanks to the students in our courses, honors students, and their friends who gave us feedback on the Net Generation Survey and who volunteered to pilot test the original version of the survey. The energy and positive outlooks of our students have been a positive influence on both of us, and we look forward to being active participants with the Net Generation as they transform student affairs.

Rey Junco

Thanks to Danny Fay, recent graduate in English from the University of Florida, who has spent countless hours editing my work, including this book. He always reminds me that I can say things much more clearly than I usually do. I look forward to his enrollment in a graduate program in public policy and his likely work on higher education issues. Danny is someone who enjoys the issues and will be an asset to the higher education community.

ix

Thanks to Lynn O'Sickey and Glenn Kepic of the University of Florida College of Liberal Arts and Sciences Academic Advising Center for giving me great stories and information about their work. Although I see many of the trends in advising, they see the typical UF students, and sometimes their stories blow me away.

Thanks to Allan Burns for including me as a faculty member in the study abroad program to the Yucatan. Without him, I would not have had the time or clarity to begin work on this project.

Thanks to our NASPA friends for routinely attending our presentations and inviting us to speak on their campuses and at other meetings.

Thanks to Rey Junco, whose diligence and drive kept me on task with this book. He's an "idea guy" who wrangles opportunities left and right, and he always includes me. I still can't believe that we never crossed paths at the University of Florida.

I'd like to thank my long-time roommate Jason Hinson for his patience and tolerance of my piles of books, papers, and articles. Thanks also to Oliver the walker hound and Lucy the dachshund, both faithful members of my household; they sometimes try to eat my words but mostly just want me to stay home with them and watch reruns of *Gilmore Girls*, *Law and Order*, and *West Wing*.

Finally, thanks to NASPA for the opportunities to present my work at the conferences and through this book.

Jeanna Mastrodicasa

FOREWORD

Most of us who were born before 1982 find the computer age both exciting and challenging. We've seen it all, from snail mail to e-mail, stereos to iPods, no net to Internet, encyclopedias to Wikipedia, land phones to cell phones, antennas to cable/satellite, typing to word processing, vacuum tubes to transistors, maps to global positioning. To varying extents, we are all forced to participate in the computer age, whether we want to or not. Some join in enthusiastically, keeping up with and using the latest technological advances, while others go along because they have no choice but to deal with computer-generated voice-recorded messages (with their many options), computer-generated bank statements, help desks in Bangladesh, and cars we can no longer fix ourselves. Many of us are not really sure if the obvious benefits of all this technology outweigh the not-so-obvious costs in both economic and human terms. So we limp along, using (and benefiting from, we think) the latest technological innovations but not really understanding either the technology or its impact on our lives.

On the other hand, those who were born in and after 1982 (the Net Generation) appear to have no such dilemmas. Technology has always been part of their lives, and they are not intimidated in the least by technological innovation. Members of the Net Generation are as much at ease with their laptops as they are with their hairdryers. They know more about computers than their parents do, and technology is simply an unquestioned part of their day-to-day existence. Because of computer technology, their brains may develop differently than those of previous generations (although in what ways is still unclear). Some people, by virtue of their privileged backgrounds, will have clear technological advantages in life over those who are less fortunate. Computer-based communication may have a mixed and as yet unknown impact on the development of interpersonal communication skills. And education may be enormously affected by the advances of the computer age.

Nowhere is the generational digital divide more apparent than in colleges and universities. In the classroom, students expect to review faculty lecture notes on the course Web page, use laptops to take notes in class, communicate with faculty using instant messaging, transmit their papers as e-mail attachments, and use search engines as valid sources of information. Faculty, on the other hand, may be unfamiliar with or even object to the use of these technological "advances" to enhance learning in their classrooms. Furthermore, students may demand the speed and efficiency of computer-based administrative systems. For example, on some campuses, it is possible to get information about the institution, apply for admission, gain acceptance, receive academic advice, and register for classes exclusively through computer-based systems; other institutions may not have the financial resources to provide such services. How students relate to one another, how they communicate, and how they use their time are strongly influenced by cell phones, text messaging, iPods, computer dating services, and computer games. College administrators may lag in their understanding of the extent and potential impact of these activities on students, for good or for ill.

Until recently, research about and discussion of the impact of technology on higher education has been sparse. While we may suspect that technology is a double-edged sword, not many of us have enough knowledge to think about or analyze the impact of technology on our students' educational experiences, let alone decide how technology should be managed to promote its upside while minimizing its downside. In this book, Reynol Junco and Jeanna Mastrodicasa fill a significant part of this informational and analytical void by defining the Net Generation and the technology its members use, reviewing research on the impact of technology on higher education (inside and outside the classroom) and on the workplace students will face upon graduation. The authors offer excellent recommendations for implementing policies and practices that enhance the positive use of technology in the collegiate setting. This book is an important addition to our understanding of higher education, student learning, campus cultures, and educational pedagogy. I learned much from these chapters, and I trust you will as well.

M. Lee Upcraft

M. Lee Upcraft is assistant vice president emeritus for student affairs, professor emeritus of higher education, and senior research scientist at the Center for the Study of Higher Education at Penn State University.

Preface

I t was March 2001, and the NASPA–Student Affairs Administrators in Higher Education Annual National Conference was under way with the usual rituals. Long-time friends and colleagues were gathered, reconnecting, and weaving their way among three conference hotels, the conference center, and fabulous Seattle restaurants. Still not caught up on sleep, thanks to hopping over three time zones, I groggily made my way to the gigantic ballroom for the keynote address. I found my friends and took a seat. The large projection screen monitors came to life, showing the hallway outside the ballroom and something extraordinary—NASPA president Shannon Ellis speeding toward the camera riding a Razor scooter. This was only my third NASPA conference, and I thought, "This is definitely a forward-looking and hip organization." Right there, zipping into the room and onto the podium, was my proof—Shannon Ellis skating around like a student on any college campus. I decided that this was one group of conference attendees who would certainly be in touch with their students.

After Ellis's introduction, Dr. Drew Pinsky, co-host of the radio-show-turned-MTV-hit *Loveline*, took the stage to deliver what was, in my opinion, one of the best NASPA keynote addresses ever. I was enthralled. As a psychologist and counselor-in-training, I knew Dr. Drew's work quite well—his role on the show was as a medical expert and unofficial "voice of reason" on sexuality issues for the current generation of young adults. I watched *Loveline* from time to time (in between research, my assistantship, and classes) and was always impressed by the gentle, matter-of-fact style he used to engage his audience and to reach the teens and young adults watching the show. I knew from talking with undergraduate students that many of them watched *Loveline* and considered Dr. Drew's advice useful.

I was thrilled to hear Dr. Drew live—so much so that I chased after him and asked if he would allow me to have a picture taken with him. That picture is still in my office, and many of my students recognize him, even though the show no longer airs on MTV. Later that day, in discussing his presentation with friends and colleagues, I was surprised to learn that many of them were not familiar with Dr. Drew, even though they were only a few years older than traditional-aged college students. I decided to engage in some anecdotal data collection. Throughout the conference, I asked as many people as I could if they had heard of Dr. Drew before they attended his presentation. Many said no, although they agreed with his views and enjoyed his speech.

I believed that I had uncovered something significant—although I didn't really know what it was. I asked my new NASPA friend Jeanna Mastrodicasa, "Can you believe most of the folks here had never heard of Dr. Drew?" She was as astonished as I was, especially as we both agreed that Dr. Drew had more influence on how college students viewed sexuality than any other person, institution, or educational resource. But we moved on and spoke about topics more pressing for two graduate students at a large national conference: the locations and times of the receptions that would offer the best free food, and when we might expect the next Beastie Boys album. We briefly talked about whether it would be possible for two young hipsters like ourselves to move the student affairs profession forward by helping educate professionals on what students are really like—what kind of music they listen to, what influences them, what their slang means, and so on.

To put this time period in its proper historical context, it is important to note the cultural markers and technological advancements since Jeanna and I spoke at the 2001 NASPA conference in Seattle. For instance,

- XM Satellite Radio started broadcasting in 2001; it now has more than 7 million subscribers (XM Satellite Radio Web site, 2006).

- Apple's iPod had not yet been released; it debuted in October 2001 (Wikipedia, 2006b).

- The terrorist attacks of September 11, 2001, had not yet occurred.

- Most members of the Net Generation were eligible to vote in their first presidential election in 2000.

- In 2001, 56% of adults and 73% of teens ages 12–17 years used the Internet, compared with 67% and 87%, respectively, in 2005 (Fallows 2005; Fox & Madden, 2005).

🗁 Among teenagers, since 2000, there has been a 38% increase in obtaining news online, a 71% increase in shopping online, and a 47% increase in obtaining health information online (Lenhart, Madden, & Hitlin, 2005).

🗁 The term "helicopter parent" was not part of the language of higher education; it did not gain popularity until student affairs professionals began using it in 2001 to describe parents who "hover" over their college-student children (Wikipedia, 2006a).

🗁 Wikipedia didn't exist.

The following year, at the 2002 NASPA conference in Boston, Jeanna and I again discussed our idea of educating fellow student affairs professionals about what was going on with students. We were more serious in our discussion this time, as we had spoken to colleagues who encouraged us to "put something together" for a NASPA presentation. We had a general sense of wanting to help student affairs professionals understand the students with whom they work, and we thought it would be fun to present something together. We both love what we do and feel a special connection with our students that may have something to do with our connections to our "inner children."

Jeanna and I submitted a proposal on the topic of the Net Generation for the 2003 NASPA conference; we were pleasantly surprised that the reviewers thought our presentation was worthy of inclusion. We realized that we had a great deal of work to do, so we arranged informal focus groups, asked students in our classes to tell us about their "culture," spoke to as many students as we could, and read all the research we could find about the Net Generation. The most surprising aspect of our presentation at the 2003 NASPA conference was the response from the workshop attendees and the national office staff. Our presentation was even mentioned during a keynote address—the theme for the conference was *It's All About the Stu-*

dents, and our presentation fit right in. The reviews were overwhelmingly positive, including comments such as "I never knew *that* about students."

Jeanna and I left the conference feeling confident that we were slowly heading toward our goal—educating student affairs professionals about the cultural nuances of their traditional-aged students. We continued to receive positive feedback from NASPA colleagues after the conference and were invited to speak to student affairs professionals and organizations. Since then, we have been fortunate to work with great students on our campuses who have taught us more about their beliefs, values, and culture than we could ever glean from formal research. We have also been fortunate to work with student affairs professionals around the country who encourage us in our research, writing, and workshops.

We hope this book will serve as a cultural guide to the Net Generation, like travel guides for people who are exploring new places. There's nothing inherently "wrong" with students from the Net Generation or with people from other generations; there are just cultural barriers that need to be understood (and overcome) to allow for the best working relationships between groups. As you read this book, set aside any preconceived notions you may have about Net Generation students (and their parents). Pretend you are learning about these people for the first time. We hope the information we present will help you understand more about your students and give you more tools to effectively communicate with them, teach them, and aid them in their development.

Reynol Junco
November 15, 2006
Boalsburg, Pennsylvania

REFERENCES

Fallows, D. (2005). *How women and men use the Internet*. Washington, DC: Pew Internet and American Life Project.

Fox, S., & Madden, M. (2005, December). Generations online. Data memo posted to Pew Internet and American Life Project Web site, Retrieved September 25, 2006, from http://www.pewinternet.org/pdfs/PIP_Generations_Memo.pdf

Lenhart, A., Madden, M., &Hitlin, P. (2005). *Teens and technology*. Washington, DC: Pew Internet and American Life Project.

Wikipedia Web site. (2006a). Helicopter parents. Retrieved September 25, 2006, from http://en.wikipedia.org/wiki/Helicopter_parent

Wikipedia Web site. (2006b). iPod. Retrieved September 25, 2006, from http://en.wikipedia.org/wiki/IPod#History_and_design

XM Satellite Radio Web site. (2006). History. Retrieved September 25, 2006, from http://www.xmradio.com/corporate_info/history_main.jsp

Chapter 1

Introduction to the Net Generation

The Net Generation includes traditional-aged college students who began arriving at institutions of higher education in 2000. The uniqueness of the Net Generation has caused student affairs professionals to focus on how these students are different from previous generations and how we can meet their needs with services and expectations (Reesor & Schlabach, 2006). Specifically, student affairs professionals are aware of the speed at which Net Generation cultural influences are communicated through the students' use of high-speed technology. In this book, we combine a review of the literature on the Net Generation, firsthand knowledge from working with these students, and our own qualitative and quantitative research to reach conclusions, articulate implications, and make recommendations for faculty and student affairs professionals.

This chapter introduces the Net Generation as a group of students with a unique shared personality that is highly influenced by the ease with which they use technology. Chapter 2 gives an overview of the technology used by these students. Chapter 3 provides a research-based picture of the Net Generation, and chapter 4 introduces the Net Generation Survey, which we created to assess how members of this generation are using technology. Chapter 4 also includes a summary of the results of our ongoing research project with Net Generation students. Chapter 5 discusses the issues facing student affairs professionals who work with these students, and chapter 6 reviews the major implications for career development and workplace issues for the Net Generation. Chapter 7 focuses on working with the Net Generation in academic advising settings, and chapter 8 covers pedagogy and working with these students in the classroom.

THE NET GENERATION ARRIVES ON CAMPUS

2

Generations of college students have affected institutions of higher education throughout history. The arrival of the latest group—the Net Generation—has triggered numerous discussions on college campuses about how to best serve these students. The Net Generation is described as having seven common traits—they are special, sheltered, confident, team-oriented, conventional, pressured, and achieving (Strauss & Howe, 2006). They are racially and ethnically diverse, interested in new technologies, prefer group activities, and identify with the values of their parents more than other young people have in the past century. The Net Generation has had a major impact on higher education (Howe and Strauss, 2000; Mastrodicasa & Junco, 2006; Reesor & Schlabach, 2006).

It is not possible to describe an entire group using broad generalities;

by attempting to describe the generation as a whole, we will miss some of the richness of intragenerational variability. The reader should remember that, for the most part, we are describing the *peer personality* of traditional-aged U.S. college students born in and after 1982. A peer personality is defined by Strauss and Howe (2006) as a common persona that results from sharing important events in a generation's history. Strauss and Howe (2006) noted that not everyone in each generation shares the peer personality; however, everyone in that generation has to deal with it.

It is important to discuss the Net Generation in relation to other living generations to understand the interactions among the generations. In this chapter we review four generations (see Figure 1.1): the Silent Generation, Boomers, Generation X, and the Net Generation. Generations are not strictly defined by dates; rather, they are grouped by coming of age around a common time and sharing a common location in history (Coomes & DeBard, 2004). Common locations in history are often defined by shared events, such as World Wars I and II, the Space Shuttle Challenger explosion in 1986, or the terrorist attacks of September 11, 2001; such events influence the peer personality of a group. For instance, persons who came of age during the Great Depression have a peer personality that includes the ability to endure hardship (Howe & Strauss, 2000; Lancaster & Stillman, 2002).

3

Literature about working with certain populations of college students who need extra support—such as first-generation college students; racial and ethnic minority students; gay, lesbian, bisexual, and transgender students; students with disabilities; student athletes; and students with at least one immigrant parent—provides detailed information about those populations. Discussions of generational trends often result in generalizations about large groups of people, but the themes that emerge can still provide guidance for higher education leaders (Terry, Dukes, Valdez, & Wilson, 2005).

Figure 1.1. An overview of the four generations.

	Silent Generation Born between 1925–1942	Boomers Born between 1943–1960	Generation X Born between 1961–1981	Net Generation Born between 1982–Now
Peer Personality	Loyal Collaborative Personal sacrifice Patriotic Conformity Respect for authority Civic pride	Optimistic Competitive Individualistic Reject authority Return to religious values	Independent Skeptical Latchkey kids Shun traditional values Nihilism	Special Sheltered Confident Conventional Team-oriented Achieving Pressured
Defining Events	WWI & II Great Depression New Deal	Vietnam War Watergate Women's Rights Reagan recession Civil Rights Movement Television	Challenger accident MTV Computers Video games Persian Gulf War	Columbine shootings September 11 attacks Oklahoma City bombing
Attended College	1943–1960	1961–1978	1979–1999	2000–Now

THE SILENT GENERATION

Born between 1925 and 1942, members of the Silent Generation (sometimes also called the Traditional or Greatest Generation) are described as loyal, seeking to reach common goals by collaborating with others and putting aside individual needs (Lancaster & Stillman, 2002; Reesor & Schlabach, 2006). The two world wars and the Great Depression had a tremendous impact on those from the Silent Generation who made personal sacrifices to sustain their lives and protect their country (Lancaster & Stillman, 2002). This group tends to believe in the ability of institutions—including government, the church, and the military—to effect change (Lancaster & Stillman, 2002). More than half of Silent Generation men are veterans; patriotism is important to this group (Lancaster &

Stillman, 2002). This generation attended college between 1943 and 1960 (Coomes & DeBard, 2004).

BOOMERS

Baby Boomers, born between 1943 and 1960 are known for being optimistic and competitive (Lancaster & Stillman, 2002; Reesor & Schlabach, 2006). A very large generation, Boomers experienced overcrowded schools and saw the creation of mass consumer goods. The early Boomers, who were much more focused on success, were labeled "yuppies" (young urban professionals). They were greatly influenced by the arrival of television in the 1950s—in 1952 there were 4 million TV sets in the United States; in 1960, there were 50 million. Television created a new set of reference points (e.g., TV shows, characters, products) for this generation that were different from those of their parents. Many events that affected the Boomers were divisive: the war in Vietnam, Watergate, the women's rights movement, and the Reagan-era economic recession (Lancaster & Stillman, 2002). The Boomers went to college in times of significant civil unrest on campus, between 1961 and 1978 (Coomes & DeBard, 2004).

5

GENERATION X

Generation Xers (born from 1961 to 1981) are considered to be skeptical and independent, calling every major U.S. institution into question—the military, the presidency, organized religion, corporate America, and marriage. People in this generation generally prefer to put more faith in themselves as individuals and to use their own resources rather than relying on institutions. They remember their childhoods as complex; the news carried stories of violence, AIDS, crack cocaine, drunk drivers, child molesters, and disappearing children. Generation Xers grew up with a range of media opportunities beyond the TV of the Boomers' generation—video games, VCRs, cable TV, fax machines, and personal computers (Lancaster & Stillman, 2002). Most Gen Xers went to college between 1979 and 1999, however, some may still be enrolled in institutions of higher education as nontraditional-aged students (Coomes & DeBard, 2004).

THE NET GENERATION

The Net Generation, whose members were born in and after 1982, is the largest generation in history, surpassing 80 million in number. This generation has several names, such as Millennials, Generation Y, and Echo Boomers (Lancaster & Stillman, 2002; see also Coomes & DeBard, 2004). We call them the Net Generation to reflect the tremendous impact the Internet and technology have had on their development. While World War II and the war in Vietnam shaped the Silent Generation and the Boomers, the integration of technology into daily life has influenced the Net Generation. From childhood they have been using cell phones and computers that keep them in constant contact with other people down the street and around the globe (Junco, 2005). Generation Xers, due to the fact that they had less parental involvement in their upbringing, were exposed to more violence in the media and they also experienced more violence in their schools. The Boomer parents of Net Generation students have emphasized personal safety in their children's upbringing and attempt to shield their children from media violence. Furthermore, the Net Generation student's focus on following the rules has led to a marked decrease in school violence (Lancaster & Stillman, 2002; Strauss & Howe, 2006).

The Net Generation's peer personality bears the closest resemblance not to their relative peers, the Gen Xers, or to their Boomer parents, but to the members of the Silent Generation. Members of the Net Generation are optimistic, value civic duty, are achievement-oriented, and respect authority. Because of these qualities, some consider the Net Generation the next great generation (Coomes & DeBard, 2004; Lancaster & Stillman, 2002;

Strauss & Howe, 2006). Howe and Strauss (2003) stated that "the most important link [the Silent Generation have] to today's teens is the void they leave behind: No other adult peer group possesses anything close to their upbeat, high-achieving, team-playing, and civic-minded reputation" (p. 22).

Members of the Net Generation are today's college students, and they are transforming the demographics of higher education enrollment in the United States. They are the most ethnically and racially diverse college group in history (Coomes & DeBard, 2004; Terry, Dukes, Valdez, & Wilson, 2005). The 2000 Census found that just over 31% of the Net Generation is from minority racial and ethnic backgrounds, and this percentage is growing. Nearly three quarters of all current undergraduates are defined as "nontraditional" by the National Center for Education Statistics (NCES), which means they have at least one of the following characteristics: "(1) delayed enrollment, (2) attend part-time, (3) work full time, (4) are financially independent, (5) have dependents, (6) are single parents, or (7) lack a high school diploma" (Oblinger, 2003, p. 38).

THE NET GENERATION'S SEVEN CORE PERSONALITY TRAITS

Neil Howe and William Strauss, best known for their book *Millennials Rising: The Next Great Generation* (2000), identified the following seven core personality traits of the Net Generation's peer personality.

Special: The first members of the Net Generation were born in the early 1980s as children of the subset of Boomer parents labeled "yuppies." Boomer dads started out by involving themselves in the childbirth process; they attended childbirth courses and were present at the births of their children. With the end of the Cold War, the national political focus was shifted to enhancing the development of children through educational systems. Enrichment programs such as Head Start became popular during this time.

Members of the Net Generation internalized a sense of specialness in part from their experience of dominating the national dialogue. They also believe they will be the generation that will help Americans realize better futures through their civic-mindedness and leadership, qualities absent in the Gen Xers, who are distrustful of and apathetic toward civic and political service (Strauss & Howe, 2006). The large size of the Net Generation has made it an important object of attention—whether from their Boomer parents telling them they are special or from companies trying to sell them products (DeBard, 2004; Howe & Strauss, 2003).

The role of Net Generation students' parents in their lives, including their college experience, is striking (DeBard, 2004; Howe & Strauss, 2003). One of the biggest shifts for college campuses has been in the relationships between students and their parents; Boomer parents are extremely involved in their children's lives and directly involved with their children's colleges. Everything that happens to Net Generation students is considered vital to their parents' sense of purpose, and their parents advocate for them throughout college and beyond (DeBard, 2004; Howe & Strauss, 2003; Keppler, Mullendore, & Carey, 2005).

Sheltered: Parents and authority figures have sheltered this generation from harm. These efforts have ranged from the innocuous "Baby on Board" signs to the serious school safety changes made in the post-Columbine era (DeBard, 2004; Howe & Strauss, 2003). Net Gen parents are concerned about their children's safety and lobby for measures such as v-chips for television sets, metal detectors and security guards in schools, and spy cameras to monitor their babysitters. Younger students from the Net Generation are comfortable with significant parental involvement in their safety, which is the opposite of the Gen Xers' experience.

The Net Generation has been encouraged to follow the rules in school and throughout their development. These students expect to be suspended from school if they possess toy guns or butter knives. They trust that their parents and authority figures will apply rules fairly (DeBard, 2004; Howe & Strauss, 2003; Strauss & Howe, 2006). Members of the Net Generation have spent their childhoods in structured, organized activities rather than in unstructured play (DeBard, 2004; Howe & Strauss, 2003). In fact, the focus on structured activities has become so rigorous that the American Academy of Pediatrics (2006) recently encouraged parents to allow their children to spend time in free play and engage in unstructured activities for the benefit of their development.

Confident: Members of the Net Generation exude optimism and expect to hear good news (DeBard, 2004; Lancaster & Stillman, 2002). Net Gen teenagers believe that they (and their children) will be able to achieve the American Dream. They believe it is easier to be a kid today than in their parents' time. They say they are optimistic about their chances of obtaining good jobs, and many believe they will be more financially successful than their parents (Strauss & Howe, 2006).

The Net Generation trusts authority figures, who have given them rewards such as trophies for participating in activities as children and scholarships for passing achievement tests in high school (DeBard, 2004; Howe & Strauss, 2000; 2003). They are good negotiators in determining acceptable levels of behavior with parents, teachers, and employers (DeBard, 2004; Zemke, Raines, & Filipczak, 2000). Net Gen students are motivated to make an effort to meet the expectations of others, and they expect beneficial outcomes (DeBard, 2004; Zemke, Raines, & Filipczak, 2000).

Conventional: The Boomer parents of the Net Generation rebelled against the conventional attitudes of their own parents. Members of the Net Generation have a stronger connection to their parents and have returned to more conventional values. Strauss and Howe (2006) report that Net Generation teenagers and young adults are more likely than any generation in history to share their parents' values.

DeBard (2004) says that members of the Net Generation have learned to go along to get along, and they prefer not to take risks or be out of compliance with social rules. The Boomers defined social rules for the Net Generation, and they have had the power and resources to support those who followed these rules. Codes of conduct, proper dress, and high-stakes proficiency testing are typical experiences of members of the Net Generation (DeBard, 2004).

Team-oriented: In contrast to the disconnectedness of Generation X, Net Generation members are more connected to each other than any previous generation. Net Gen students like to congregate, whether in person, on cell phones, or on the Internet (DeBard, 2004). They seek out technology that helps them stay connected, such as instant messaging and social networking Web sites like Facebook. Teachers have capitalized on the idea of students influencing each other in positive ways by having them work in groups and on academic teams. Academic teamwork is so common that Net Gen students prefer to work in teams on academic projects because they feel less individual pressure (DeBard, 2004).

Throughout their childhoods, Net Generation children participated in activities such as team sports and youth programs (Howe & Strauss, 2000; 2003; Strauss & Howe, 2006; Terry, Dukes, Valdez, & Wilson, 2005). They like to cooperate with others and want to be perceived by authority figures as willing to work in groups (DeBard, 2004). At the same time, Net Gen students are uncomfortable with controversy and look to authority figures to protect them in periods of conflict (Lancaster & Stillman, 2002; see also DeBard, 2004).

Achieving: The Net Generation is the highest-achieving generation in history (DeBard, 2004). Average SAT scores have increased 18 points from 1995–2005 and high school students report having definitive long-term plans that include specific college choices and career directions (College Board, 2006). On the one hand, these students are serious about preparing for their careers; on the other hand, they report liking school less than previous generations did. Net Generation students are scoring much better in math and science, and are following career paths along those lines (Strauss & Howe, 2006).

In addition to the real achievements of these students, grade inflation has increased dramatically in the past 30 years, according to data from the Cooperative Institute Research Project (CIRP; Astin, Oseguera, Sax, & Korn, 2002). For instance, in the late 1960s, 20.7% of students reported earning grades of C+ or below in high school while only 17.7% of students reported earning grades of A- or higher. Since the late 60s, there has been a steady shift in the balance to where grades of A- or higher drastically outnumber grades of C+ or less. In 2003, 46.6% of students reported A grades while only 5.1% reported C grades! One of the two periods that saw the most drastic change in grade inflation was the time between 1986 and 2003, during the time the Net Generation have attended high school (Sax, Astin, Lindholm, Korn, Saens, & Mahoney, 2004). High school grade inflation has caused Net Generation students to believe they will do better in college than those from other generations. Indeed, the percentage of entering first-year students who expected to earn a "B" in college has jumped from 26.7% in the 1960s to 57.5% in 2001 (Astin, Oseguera, Sax, & Korn, 2002).

Pressured: In addition to having an achievement focus, members of the Net Generation feel pressure to perform in part due to their focus on achievement (DeBard, 2004). They believe that their long-term success hinges on the choices they make today; to them, success comes from a combination of planning and effort. In this sense, Net Gen students feel a lot of pressure to do well on their exams and in other forms of evaluation (Strauss & Howe, 2006). High school students are aware that getting into college requires more than just good grades, so they fill their schedules with extracurricular activities.

11

Stress and anxiety are common traits of Net Generation college students (Terry, Dukes, Valdez, & Wilson, 2005). The percentage of college students who reported depression and anxiety in "the last school year" on the American College Health Association (ACHA) National College Health Assessment survey increased steadily from 2000 to 2005 (American College Health Association, 2006). In 2000, 16% of students reported experiencing depression in the previous school year and 7% reported experiencing anxiety while in 2005, the figures were 21% and 14%, respectively. DeBard (2004) believes this anxiety is due to the fact that the Boomers push their Net Generation children to succeed to show how good their parenting skills are and for their own sense of accomplishment. Another possible reason for the increase in mental health issues is that Net Generation college students feel pressured by their parents and by themselves to succeed.

Net Generation students are much different from their counterparts in previous generations. Their arrival on college campuses signals a return to more conventional values reminiscent of the Silent Generation era. Also, these students' connections to each other and the world via technology are unique. The world in which they have developed has cherished them as America's next great generation and has provided them with technological tools unlike any ever seen. Their comfort with these technologies will continue to shape their own and future generations. Throughout this book, we discuss the influence on the Net Generation of these core personality traits and of technology.

References

American Academy of Pediatrics. (2006). The importance of play in promoting healthy child development and maintaining strong parent-child bonds. Retrieved November 12, 2006, from http://www.aap.org/pressroom/playFINAL.pdf

American College Health Association. (2006). National College Health Assessment Web Summary. Retrieved October 4, 2006, from http://www.acha.org/projects_programs/ncha_sampledata.cfm

Astin, A. W., Oseguera, L., Sax, L. J., & Korn, W. S. (2002). *The American freshman: Thirty-five year trends*. Los Angeles: Higher Education Research Institute.

College Board. (2006). *2006 College-bound seniors: Total group profile report*. Retrieved January 23, 2007 from http://www.collegeboard.com/prod_downloads/about/news_info/cbsenior/yr2006/national-report.pdf

Coomes, M. D., & DeBard, R. (2004). A generational approach to understanding students. In M. D. Coomes & R. DeBard (Eds.), *Serving the millennial generation: New directions for student services, no.106* (pp. 5–16). San Francisco: Jossey-Bass.

DeBard, R. (2004). Millennials coming to college. In M. D. Coomes & R. DeBard (Eds.), *Serving the millennial generation: New directions for student services, no. 106* (pp. 33–45). San Francisco: Jossey-Bass.

Howe, N., & Strauss, W. (2000). *Millennials rising: The next great generation*. New York: Vintage Books.

Howe, N., & Strauss, W. (2003). *Millennials go to college*. Great Falls, VA: American Association of Registrars and Admissions Officers and Life-Course Associates.

Junco, R. (2005). Technology and today's first-year students. In M. L. Upcraft, J. N. Gardner, B. O. Barefoot, & associates (Eds.), *Meeting*

13

challenges and building support: Creating a climate for first-year student success (pp. 221–238). San Francisco: Jossey-Bass.

Keppler, K., Mullendore, R. H., & Carey, A. (2005). *Partnering with the parents of today's college students.* Washington, DC: National Association of Student Personnel Administrators.

Lancaster, L.C., & Stillman, D. (2002). *When generations collide.* New York: Harper Collins.

Mastrodicasa, J., & Junco, R. (2006, May 10). How to meet millennials' expectations (part 1). *NetResults.* Retrieved September 29, 2006, from http://www.naspa.org/membership/mem/nr/article.cfm?id=1533

Oblinger, D. (2003). Boomers, Gen-Xers, & Millennials: Understanding the new students. *EDUCAUSE Review,* 37–47.

Reesor, L., & Schlabach, K. (2006, Fall). Managing multi-generations: Strategies for crossing the generational divide in the workplace. *Leadership Exchange, 4*(3), 16–19.

Sax, L. J., Astin, A.W., Lindholm, J.A., Korn, W.S., Saens, V.B., & Mahoney, K.M. (2004). The American freshman: National norms for Fall 2003. Los Angeles: Higher Education Research Institute.

Strauss, W. & Howe, N. (2006). *Millennials and the pop culture: Strategies for a new generation of consumers in music, movies, television, the Internet, and video games.* Great Falls, VA: LifeCourse Associates.

Terry, R. B., Dukes, C. M., Valdez, L. E., & Wilson, A. (2005). Changing demographics and diversity in higher education. In K. Keppler., R. H. Mullendore, & A. Carey (Eds.), *Partnering with the parents of today's college students*. Washington, DC: National Association of Student Personnel Administrators.

United States Census (2000). Total population by age, race, and Hispanic or Latino origin for the United States: 2000. Retrieved November 5, 2006, from http://www.census.gov/population/cen2000/phc-t9/tab01.pdf

Zemke, R., Raines, C., & Filipczak, B. (2000). *Generations at work: Managing the clash of Veterans, Boomers, Xers, and Nexters in your workplace.* New York: American Management Association.

Chapter 2

Technology Used by the Net Generation

The Net Generation is the most technologically advanced group of students ever to enroll in college. They arrive on campus having been consumers of high-speed technology in ways that previous generations barely understand. Net Generation students are comfortable with and use a wide range of technologically advanced tools to enhance their lives. Today's college students are at ease with bleeding-edge technologies—technologies that have not yet proven themselves as stable, useful, or viable but that have a great deal of potential (Wikipedia, 2006). In this chapter, we review some of the more popular technologies used by the Net Generation, including instant messaging, text messaging, blogs, Facebook, MySpace, and file sharing.

An important caveat is that changes in technology occur at a lightning pace, so the technologies reviewed in this chapter will evolve rapidly and their popularity with Net Gen students will wax and wane. It's possible—even likely—that some or all of the technologies we review here will be replaced by emerging technologies. One thing is certain: The Net Generation will continue to adopt new technologies quickly and expertly.

INSTANT MESSAGING

Instant messaging (IM) software allows for real-time (synchronous) communication with friends on a "buddy list." Users of IM programs are shown a list of their friends who are online; they can click on names to send messages. A box pops up on the friend's computer screen. It includes the message and space to enter a reply. Back-and-forth instant messaging is called "chatting" because of the interactive, real-time nature of the communication (Junco, 2005).

18

Members of the Net Generation are far more likely to IM than people from other generations. A Pew Internet and American Life Project survey found that 62% of the Net Generation used IM, compared with 37% of Generation Xers (Shiu & Lenhart, 2004). Furthermore, IM is such an ingrained part of Net Generation members' lives that they can easily do other things at the same time. The Pew study found that 49% of those in the Net Generation multitasked while using IM, compared with 32% of Generation Xers. The percentage of those who report multitasking while using IM—or using it at all—declines with each previous generation (Shiu & Lenhart, 2004).

Instant messaging allows Net Gen students to communicate easily. Lenhart, Rainie, and Lewis (2001) found that 19% of teenagers used IM as the primary method to contact their friends; 17% used it to ask someone out on a date; and 13% had used IM to end a relationship. Of particular note was the finding that 37% of teenagers had used IM to communicate something they would not have said in person.

College students have a wide variety of freely available programs that allow them to engage in instant messaging; however, most college students in the United States use the AOL application (see chapter 4). Like other IM software, AOL's service allows users to select screen names (handles) by which they appear to others on their buddy lists. IM software allows users to send files and is often used for transmitting photos. Additionally, IM software has an "away message" feature that serves as a digital answering machine. College students use the away message to let their buddies know what they're doing and to communicate news, gossip, and contact information. (See chapter 4 for a discussion of how students use away messages.)

Text Messaging

Text messaging (texting) is the use of cell phones or cellular-enabled devices (such as handheld devices) to send and receive short messages; it is similar to IM or e-mail. (In Europe, texting is referred to as SMS, or short messaging service.) Text messages are entered into cell phones using the number pad. For example, to type the letter "M," one must press the "6" key three times. Because it takes so long to type messages in proper English, a form of slang has developed for texting. Some of these abbreviations have "crossed over" and are also used in instant messaging. Table 2.1 lists some frequently used abbreviations for text messaging.

Net Generation students are very comfortable with texting and use it frequently. In fact, they are moving away from conventional forms of communication. In a survey of undergraduates at a large research university, Mastrodicasa and Kepic (2005) found that 97.2% of students owned cell phones and 66.7% did not have land lines in their homes. College student

19

cell phone owners were frequent users of text messaging: 57.4% reported that they text messaged at least once a day, and 7.1% reported that they text messaged more than seven times a day (Mastrodicasa & Kepic, 2005). Members of this generation are much more comfortable with emerging communication technologies than they are with traditional forms of communication.

Table 2.1. **Text message abbreviations and explanations.**

Abbreviation	Meaning	Abbreviation	Meaning
404	I don't know	BAU	business as usual
AAR	at any rate	BBIAF	be back in a few
AAS	alive and smiling	BBIAM	be back in a minute
ADD	address	BBL	be back later
AND	any day now	BBS	be back soon
AFAIK	as far as I know	BC	because
AFK	away from keyboard	BCNU	be seein' you
AISB	as it should be	BF	best friend
AKA	also known as	BFN	bye for now
AML	all my love	BG	big grin
AOTA	all of the above	BGWM	be gentle with me
ASAP	as soon as possible	BFG	big fucking grin
A/S/L	age/sex/location	BLNT	better luck next time
ASL	age/sex/location	BM&Y	between me and you
AYEC	at your earliest convenience	BOL	best of luck
AYOR	at your own risk	BRB	be right back
B/F	boyfriend	BRT	be right there
B4	before	BTA	but then again
B4N	bye for now	BTDT	been there, done that
BAU	business as usual	BTW	by the way
B4N	bye for now	BBIAF	be back in a few

Abbreviation	Meaning	Abbreviation	Meaning
BBIAM	be back in a minute	CYA	see ya
BBL	be back later	CYO	see you online
BBS	be back soon	D/L	download
BC	because	DL	download
BCNU	be seein' you	DEGT	don't even go there
BF	best friend	DIKU	Do I know you?
BFN	bye for now	DQMOT	don't quote me on this
BG	big grin	DTS	don't think so
BGWM	be gentle with me	DV8	deviate
BFG	big fucking grin	EG	evil grin
BLNT	better luck next time	EMA	e-mail address
BM&Y	between me and you	EMFBI	excuse me for butting in
BOL	best of luck	EOD	end of day
BRB	be right back	EZY	easy
BRT	be right there	F2F	face to face
BTA	but then again	F2T	free to talk
BTDT	been there, done that	FBM	fine by me
BTW	by the way	FICCL	frankly, I couldn't care less
CMON	come on	FOMCL	falling off my chair laughing
COS	because	FITB	fill in the blank
CR8	create	FRT	for real though
CRB	come right back	FWIW	for what it's worth
CRBT	crying really big tears	FYEO	for your eyes only
CU	see you	FYI	for your information
CUA	see you around	G	grin
CUL	see you later	G/F	girlfriend
CUL8R	see you later	G2CU	good to see you
CWYL	chat with you later	G2G	got to go

Abbreviation	Meaning	Abbreviation	Meaning
G2R	got to run	HAND	have a nice day
G9	genius	HF	have fun
GA	go ahead	HHIS	head hanging in shame
GAL	get a life	HOAS	hold on a second
GB	goodbye	HRU	How are you?
GBU	God bless you	HTH	hope this helps
GDR	grinning, ducking, and running	HV	have
GD/R	grinning, ducking, and running	IAC	in any case
GFI	go for it	IB	I'm back
GG	gotta go/good game	IC	I see
GIAR	give it a rest	ICBW	it could be worse
GL	good luck	IDK	I don't know
GL/HF	good luck, have fun	IDTS	I don't think so
GMTA	great minds think alike	IDUNNO	I don't know
GOI	get over it	IG2R	I've got to run
GOL	giggling out loud	IIRC	if I remember correctly
GR8	great	ILBL8	I'll be late
GR&D	grinning, running, and ducking	ILU	I love you
GT	good try	ILY	I love you
GTG	got to go	IM	instant message
GTRM	going to read mail	IMHO	in my humble opinion
H&K	hugs & kisses	IMNSHO	in my not so humble opinion
H2CUS	hope to see you soon	IMO	in my opinion
H8	hate	IMS	I am sorry
HAGN	have a good night	IOW	in other words
HAGO	have a good one	IRL	in real life

Abbreviation	Meaning	Abbreviation	Meaning
IRMC	I rest my case	M8	mate
IUSS	if you say so	MFI	mad for it
IYKWIM	if you know what I mean	MorF	male or female?
IYO	in your opinion	MOS	mother over shoulder
IYSS	if you say so	MSG	message
j00r	your	MTF	more to follow
JAC	just a sec	MTFBWU	may the force be with you
JIC	just in case	MUSM	miss you so much
JJA	just joking around	MYOB	mind your own business
JK	just kidding	N00b	newbie
JMO	just my opinion	N1	nice one
JP	just playing	NBD	no big deal
k/b	keyboard	NE	any
KIT	keep in touch	NE1	anyone
KOTC	kiss on the cheek	NFM	none for me/not for me
KOTL	kiss on the lips	NLT	no later than
KNIM	Know what I mean?	NM	nothing much/never mind
l33t	elite	NMH	not much here
L8R	later	NO1	no one
LD	later, dude/long distance	NOYB	none of your business
LERK	leaving, easy reach of keyboard	NP	no problem
LMAO	laughing my ass off	NRN	No response/reply necessary
LOL	laughing out loud	NVM .	never mind
LTM	laughing to myself	NW	no way
LTNS	long time no see	NWO	no way out
LYLAS	love you like a sis	OIC	oh, I see

23

Abbreviation	Meaning	Abbreviation	Meaning
OMG	oh my God	PRT	party
OMW	On my way	PRW	people/parents are watching
OO	over and out	PTMM	please tell me more
OOH	out of here	PXT	please explain that
OOTD	one of these days	PU	that stinks!
OP	on the phone	Q	queue
OTB	off to bed	QIK	quick
OTL	out to lunch	QT	cutie
OTOH	on the other hand	RL	real life
OTT	over the top	RME	rolling my eyes
OTTOMH	off the top of my head	ROFL	rolling on floor laughing
OTW	off to work	ROTFL	tolling on the floor laughing
OVA	over	ROTFLMAO	rolling on the floor laughing my ass off
PCM	please call me	ROTFLUTS	rolling on the floor laughing, unable to speak
PDQ	pretty darn quick	RSN	real soon now
PLMK	please let me know	RTFM	read the fucking manual
PLS	please	RUOK	Are you okay?
PLZ	please	SAL	such a laugh
PM	private message	SC	stay cool
PMFI	pardon me for interrupting	SETE	smiling ear-to-ear
PMFJI	pardon me for jumping in	SICNR	sorry, I couldn't resist
POAHF	put on a happy face	SIG2R	sorry, I've got to run
POS	parent over shoulder	SIS	snickering in silence
PPL	people	SIT	stay in touch
PROLLY	probably	SLAP	sounds like a plan

Abbreviation	Meaning	Abbreviation	Meaning
SMHID	scratching my head in disbelief	TGIF	thank God it's Friday
SNAFU	situation normal: all fouled up	THX	thanks
SO	significant other	THNX	thanks
SOL	sooner or later	THNQ	thank you
SOMY	Sick of me yet?	TIA	thanks in advance
SOTMG	short of time, must go	TIAD	tomorrow is another day
SPK	speak	TLK2UL8R	talk to you later
SPST	same place, same time	TMB	text me back
SRY	sorry	TMI	too much information
SS	so sorry	TMOT	trust me on this
SSDD	same stuff, different day	TMWFI	take my word for it
SSINF	so stupid it's not funny	TNSTAAFL	there's no such thing as a free lunch
STR8	straight	TPM	tomorrow p.m.
STW	search the Web	TPTB	the powers that be
SUITM	see you in the morning	TSTB	the sooner, the better
SUL	see you later	TTFN	ta-ta for now
SUP	What's up?	TTTT	these things take time
SYL	see you later	TTYL	talk to you later
T+	think positively	TTYS	talk to you soon
TA	thanks a lot	TU	thank you
TAFN	that's all for now	TY	thank you
TAM	tomorrow a.m.	TYT	take your time
TBD	to be determined	TYVM	thank you very much
TBH	to be honest	UGTBK	you've got to be kidding
TC	take care	UKTR	you know that's right

25

Abbreviation	Meaning	Abbreviation	Meaning
UR	your/you're	WU?	What's up?
UV	unpleasant visual	WUCIWUG	what you see is what you get
UW	you're welcome	WUF?	Where are you from?
WAM	wait a minute	WWYC	write when you can
WAN2TLK	want to talk	WYLEI	when you least expect it
WAYF	Where are you from?	WYSIWYG	what you see is what you get
W/B	write back	X	kiss
WB	welcome back	XLNT	excellent
WIIFM	What's in it for me?	YA	your
WK	week	YBS	you'll be sorry
WKD	weekend	YGBKM	you've got to be kidding me
WOMBAT	waste of money, brains, and time	YKWYCD	you know what you can do
WRK	Work	YMMV	your mileage may vary
WRUD	What are you doing?	YR	your
WTF	what the fuck	YW	you're welcome
WTG	way to go	ZZZZ	sleeping
WTH	What the heck?		

Source: Adapted from Webopedia (2006).

One author (Junco) recalls an interaction with a Net Generation student who was experiencing severe difficulties with writing. One day, at the conclusion of a meeting, the student said she had to text message someone. She took out her cell phone and quickly wrote a fairly long text message using predictive text input, in which the phone's software "guesses" the word the user is trying to type and the user has to either select the word given or scroll through a list to find the correct word. Junco commented on how amazing it was that she could use predictive input so easily even though she was having such difficulty with grammar, and the student just shrugged.

Blogs

Blogging is the act of writing in Web-based journals known as weblogs or blogs. Blogging generally involves posting information in a sequential series of dated entries like a journal. One major difference between a paper journal and a blog is that blog information is posted in a public or semipublic forum. Students from the Net Generation are especially comfortable posting personal information on their blogs, which comes as a surprise to those from other generations who are less comfortable with putting their private lives on exhibition. A cursory review of the data collected in the Net Generation Survey revealed that most blog postings by students consist of accounts of daily events; however, students also post very intimate and private details about their lives.

Blogging has been widely adopted by Net Generation students and, in fact, is increasingly popular among all segments of the population. In a 20-month period in 2003–04, blog readership increased from 11% to 27% nationwide (Rainie, 2005). As with other forms of technology, there are striking differences in blog ownership and readership between members of the Net Generation and members of other generations. Data from the Pew Internet and American Life Project revealed that adults own and read blogs less than teenagers ages 15–17, and that teenage girls own and read blogs more than teenage boys (Lenhart & Madden, 2005). Mastrodicasa and Kepic (2005) found that while college students own blogs at rates similar to those of 15–17-year-olds, many more college students than teenagers and adults read blogs. More than 63% of college students read blogs, and more than 18% have their own blogs, compared with 27% and 7% for adults, respectively; 34% and 15% for teenage boys, respectively; and 53% and 25% for teenage girls, respectively (Lenhart & Madden, 2005).

27

Data from other studies support the popularity of blogs in the Net Generation. A Pew Internet and American Life Project study found that LiveJournal.com, a Web site that allows users to post free blogs, received its highest proportion of traffic (20%) from university computers (Rainie, Kalehoff, & Hess, 2002). Additionally, data provided by LiveJournal.com show that almost all of its users are between 14 and 29 years old, and that the majority are ages 15–26, falling well within the Net Generation.

FACEBOOK

A popular Web site for Net Generation college students is Facebook (http://www.facebook.com), a social networking Web site that allows people to post profiles and add friends to those profiles (see Figure 2.1). The profiles include information such as date of birth, age, contact information, hobbies, majors, enrolled courses, favorite movies, clubs, and so on. Users can exchange messages, invite each other to join groups and attend parties, and share photos. Unlike MySpace, another popular social networking Web site, a person must be in your network to view your profile. For instance, a user with a university e-mail address will only be able to view profiles of users from the same university while someone without a university e-mail address will not be able to view the profiles of university users. Facebook also supports high school, business, and geographic social networks through which high school students, employees, and those in similar geographic regions can connect in a comparable fashion as university users.

Facebook was founded in February 2004 (Facebook, 2006) and has quickly grown in popularity among college students. As of September 2006, it was the seventh most frequently visited Web site in the United States and had more than 9.5 million registered users, over two thirds of whom logged in daily (Facebook, 2006). It is the top photo site on the Internet, with more than 1.5 million photos uploaded each day (Facebook,

2006). Data from a survey by Mastrodicasa and Kepic (2005) show that 85.5% of students at the research university they studied had accounts on Facebook; this is congruent with data provided by other sources (e.g., Arrington, 2006; see chapter 4).

Because of the instant popularity of Facebook, student affairs professionals have struggled to keep up with the trend. Only recently have college administrators started to discuss the "Facebook problem," referring to inappropriate uses of this and similar sites. Like other tools on the bleeding edge, Facebook has been adopted quickly by the Net Generation, and some people use it inappropriately, for example:

- posting pictures and statements showing engagement in illegal activities, including underage drinking;

- posting intentionally slanderous information about others, including students, faculty, and staff;

- engaging in and exacerbating disputes exclusively in an online forum; and

- posting lewd photographs of themselves or their peers.

29

But although some students use Facebook in ways that violate university rules and community standards, most use it appropriately. Facebook can be a useful tool for helping students connect with each other, their institutions, and student affairs professionals. Furthermore, college administrators can use Facebook as a way to reach students. One thing is certain: Students will not stop using Facebook and similar sites, because they give them something they want—an easier way to connect in a disconnected world. In that sense, Facebook is a paradox: an attempt by the Net Generation to connect with people using the same medium that may have increased their disconnection from others in the first place.

Figure 2.1. **Example of a Facebook profile page.**

Source: http://www.facebook.com

The popular media have reported on the dangers and nefarious uses of Facebook, including students posting sexually suggestive photos and photos of drug use and, especially, underage drinking. But a study by Watson, Smith, and Driver (2006) paints a different picture. These researchers examined the Facebook profile pictures of students at higher education institutions in 50 states and used photographic analysis to categorize each picture. They found that only 9% of profile pictures included alcohol use and only 2.7% could be considered sexually suggestive.

MYSPACE

The popularity of MySpace (http://www.myspace.com), another social networking Web site, has greatly increased in the past few years. In mid-2006, MySpace became the most-visited Web site in the United States, according to Hitwise (2006), an Internet monitoring firm. Originally a counterculture networking site strongly slanted toward promoting music, MySpace is attracting more of a mainstream audience, with about 250,000 people registering for profiles every day (Norris, 2006). MySpace works much like Facebook—users post profiles and invite others to be part of their networks. Friends are displayed on profiles just as they are on Facebook. MySpace users also can join groups and connect with their favorite national, local, or unsigned musical artists. The success of the site has come from word of mouth rather than traditional advertising—a phenomenon last seen when MTV arrived on the scene (Norris, 2006).

Over the past few years, MySpace has enabled a number of little-known bands to reach larger audiences than would otherwise have been possible. Some of these bands have obtained major record deals; for example, Fall Out Boy, the Click Five, Dashboard Confessional, Hollywood Undead, and the All-American Rejects. All these bands reached high levels of popularity by having friends connect to them and spread the word on MySpace. For the music industry—which has seen a large decline in sales

31

over the past six years—the publicity on MySpace has been a welcome boost.

In befriending artists, MySpace users can communicate directly with their favorite performers. One artist who is popular with the Net Generation is comedian Dane Cook. In September 2006, Cook had 1.5 million friends on MySpace (Dane Cook, 2006). Artists such as Cook can promote up-coming performances using the calendar feature built into MySpace. They can also post their songs (or comedy tracks) so users can listen to them or add them to their own MySpace profile pages with the click of a button. Artists (and other users) can also send bulletins to all their MySpace friends at once; these bulletins are often used to announce new releases or performance dates.

There are three major differences between Facebook and MySpace. Although Facebook has recently changed its rules about membership allowing anyone with a valid e-mail address to join, Facebook places restrictions on who can view certain profiles. For instance, only individuals from the same university may view a university user's profile. In contrast, MySpace allows users to see everyone else's profile unless a user has turned on privacy settings. The media have published stories of teenagers and college students being tricked into bad situations by predators using MySpace. This kind of media coverage, coupled with a fear of new methods of communication, has made some people think MySpace is inherently evil.

MySpace has attracted the attention of the popular media because of some of the isolated yet disturbing issues that have arisen from people posting personal information online and how it was used by those with criminal intent. An investigation by *Wired News* reporter Kevin Poulsen (2006) found 744 sex offenders registered as users on MySpace. Indeed, the potential for negative consequences when posting in such a public forum is high; but while dangers exist, some of the more common consequences may only be bruised egos or heartbreak. A student recounted this story to the authors:

It was my first week at college, and I had just recently signed up for a membership on MySpace. I was always very shy and never really good at making friends, so I figured online would be a good way to meet some people. I was browsing through locals (locals to me is anyone in the surrounding states) and I came across a picture that grabbed my attention immediately. The boy in the picture had a green mohawk that must have been close to a foot tall. He had the cheesiest grin and I knew that I had to talk to this interesting character. Although I never expected him to respond, I left him a comment, letting him know his mohawk was what caught my attention. A few days later, he returned the comment with something along the lines of "Your beautiful smile and bright blue eyes are what first caught MY attention." With just one simple comment, he basically had me in the palm of his hand.

I found out his name was Rob. We talked online for about two weeks and eventually talked on the phone, once a week or so. He had a deep voice and a southern accent that was to die for. I found myself becoming more and more attracted to him. He was polite, funny, caring, and super sweet. He would always compliment me and find ways to make me laugh. We had so much in common and could relate to each other on every level. We made plans to meet while I was on break from school. Later he told me something had come up and we wouldn't be able to get together that week. I was devastated but convinced myself we'd eventually meet. From then on, I started to catch him in one lie after another. He couldn't keep his stories straight, and he kept making up reasons for why we couldn't meet. Occasionally, I would call him and the person who would answer his phone didn't sound like him.

Whoever it was sounded like a female trying to disguise her voice and was always very quick to get off the phone. Eventually I questioned Rob, asking him if he really was who he said he was. He got angry with me and yelled at me for ever doubting him. His anger toward me made me question his identity even more.

He had sent another one of our friends an e-mail, confessing that he wasn't who he said he was. In fact, he was really a she. Cindy, not Rob. The male I had spoken to on the phone was a friend of Cindy's, and the pictures I had seen online were pictures of her best friend. As it turns out, Cindy wasn't very good at making friends either and turned to the Internet to find friendship and attention. Cindy was not comfortable with putting her pictures online, so she borrowed her friend's pictures and changed her identity. For some reason, she felt like she would get more attention if she posed as a young, good-looking male rather than as a young overweight female.

Needless to say, I have stopped talking to "Rob," but I didn't let this experience stop me from meeting people online. I met my current boyfriend online a little over six months ago and things couldn't be better.

While stories about predators abound, few stories are written about how MySpace allows people to connect with each other, express their feelings, and participate in a new kind of economy based on social connections. For example, a faculty member moved his family to a new community over the summer, enduring cries of woe and despair from his eighth-grade daughter who did not want to be uprooted. His daughter went online to find classmates at her new school; the weekend before the school year began, she attended a back-to-school party hosted by classmates with whom she had connected on MySpace. (Her parents ensured her safety by monitoring the online exchange and accompanying her to the gathering to meet her new classmates.) Most of the 90-million-plus MySpace users (Norris, 2006) are on the Web site for legitimate purposes.

The second major difference between Facebook and MySpace is that MySpace allows users to post blogs. The MySpace blog function is becoming more popular than some of the other blog-hosting Web sites, such as Blogger and LiveJournal. MySpace includes all the features of other blog-hosting sites—such as the ability to comment on a blog and Really Simple Syndication (RSS) feeds (a service that allows subscribers to have blog updates posted to their Web pages or to special reader software on their desktops). It also includes some MySpace-specific features, such as the ability to subscribe directly to each other's blogs and to form blog groups.

The third difference between Facebook and MySpace is that MySpace allows users to customize their Web pages. Users can change the colors, font styles, and backgrounds of their pages in much the same way as is done on regular Web sites. This allows users to feel a sense of ownership about their pages. In addition to visual customization, users can add free audio clips from bands that have MySpace pages.

FILE SHARING

Students from the Net Generation are avid downloaders of music and video—much more so than people from previous generations. A full 51% of teenagers 15 to 17 years old download music, and 31% download video; only 18% and 14%, respectively, of adults do so (Lenhart & Madden, 2005). Data from the Net Generation survey (see chapter 4) also indicate high rates of downloading music and video through file-sharing services.

File-sharing software allows users to distribute files to a large network of other downloaders. Most file sharing is referred to as peer-to-peer sharing, because the files are located on private computers and people use their own Internet connections to share them (as opposed to uploading files on servers that would then use their own bandwiths to distribute them). Peer-to-peer file sharing grew rapidly in popularity after Napster, the original online music-sharing service, was shut down because of lawsuits brought by the Recording Industry Association of America that alleged Napster servers stored information on files and Internet Protocol (IP) addresses of users and allowed downloaders easy access to the information. Current peer-to-peer networking software does not include centralized servers that keep IP and file information. Furthermore, current peer-to-peer software is usually freeware; that is, software that developers give away.

A number of peer-to-peer networks are available, and each one can be accessed by a multitude of software clients. Some of the more popular networks for the Net Generation include the Gnutella network (with clients such as BearShare, Grokster, and Limewire); the Ares network (with the Ares client); and BitTorrent (with clients such as Azureus, Transmission, and μTorrent). All the software share key features, including the following:

- ☐ Functions for searching files shared by others on the network

- ☐ One-click access to download files from another person's computer

- ☐ The ability to share certain folders or files on the users' hard drives

- ☐ Indicators of what is being up- or downloaded, and the up-/download speeds

- ☐ Network status

Net Generation students who share files often do not consider the implications of copyright infringement. (This topic is discussed in chapter 8.)

Summary

Net Generation students use a range of technology tools as part of their everyday lives. These students seek out new technologies to enhance their psychosocial development. Net Generation students use IM software to communicate with each other. In fact, they perceive instant messaging as conversation—a Net Generation student may refer to "talking with" friends when she was actually using IM. These students use text messaging as a quick way to communicate with one another when they do not have ready access to IM and do not want to make a phone call. They use blogs to reach many friends (and strangers) at once. Their affinity for social networking has moved into the virtual domain with their heavy use of Web sites such as Facebook and MySpace. Lastly, Net Generation students use file sharing to trade and obtain various media files for free.

The technologies Net Generation students use are value-neutral; that is, they are neither "good" nor "bad." However, these students may use the technologies in ways that are either beneficial or detrimental to their academic or psychological well-being. In chapter 3 we discuss how Net Generation students use these technologies in ways that enhance or detract from their quality of life.

37

REFERENCES

Arrington, M. (2006, September 7). 85% of college students use Facebook. Retrieved September 27, 2006, from http://www.techcrunch.
com/2005/09/07/85-of-college-students-use-facebook

Dane Cook Web site. (2006). Homepage. Retrieved September 27, 2006,
from http://www.danecook.com

Facebook Web site. (2006). Press: Facebook overview. Retrieved September
27, 2006, from http://lhup.facebook.com/press.php

Hitwise (2006). Myspace moves into #1 position for all Internet sites.
Retrieved September 27, 2006, http://weblogs.hitwise.com/bill-
tancer/2006/07/myspace_moves_into_1_position.html

Junco, R. (2005). Technology and today's first-year students. In M. L.
Upcraft, J. N. Gardner, B. O. Barefoot, & associates (Eds.), *Meeting
challenges and building support: Creating a climate for first-year student
success* (pp. 221-238). San Francisco: Jossey-Bass.

Lenhart, A., & Madden, M. (2005). *Teen content creators and consumers*.
Washington, DC: Pew Internet and American Life Project.

Lenhart, A., Rainie, L., & Lewis, O. (2001). *Teenage life online: The rise of the
instant-message generation and the Internet's impact on friendships and
family relationships*. Washington, DC: Pew Internet and American Life
Project.

Mastrodicasa, J. M., & Kepic, G. (2005, October). *Parents gone wild*. Paper
presented at the meeting of the National Academic Advising Association,
Las Vegas, NV.

Norris, M. (Host). (2006, July 12). The ascendance of MySpace. *All things
considered* [radio broadcast]. Washington, DC: National Public Radio.

Poulsen, K. (October 16, 2006). MySpace predator caught by code. *Wired*

News. Retrieved November 13, 2006, http://www.wired.com/news/technology/0,71948-0.html?tw=wn_index_1

Rainie, L. (2005, January). The state of blogging. Data memo retrieved September 26, 2006, from http://www.pewinternet.org/pdfs/PIP_blogging_data.pdf

Rainie, L., Kalehoff, M., & Hess, D. (2002, September). College students and the web. Data retrieved September 26, 2006, from http://www.pewinternet.org/pdfs/PIP_College_Memo.pdf

Shiu, E., & Lenhart, A. (2004). *How Americans use instant messaging.* Washington, DC: Pew Internet and American Life Project.

Watson, S. W., Smith, Z., & Driver, J. (2006). Alcohol, sex, and illegal activities: An analysis of selected Facebook central photos in 50 states. Educational Resources Information Center (ERIC) database online submission.

Webopedia. (2006, June). Text messaging abbreviations. Retrieved September 26, 2006, from http://www.webopedia.com/quick_ref/textmessage-abbreviations.asp

Wikipedia. (2006). Bleeding edge. Retrieved September 26, 2006, from http://en.wikipedia.org/wiki/Bleeding_edge

CHAPTER 3

Research on the Net Generation and How Technology Influences Student Development

m embers of the Net Generation, as a group, have never known a time without a World Wide Web or more importantly for them, instant messaging or cell phones. The consequences of growing up in this connected, digital world include having neural pathways that are wired differently than the pathways of people from previous generations (Prensky, 2001). In this chapter, we review the research on the Net Generation—their shared characteristics and how they are different from other generations in U.S. history. We also review the research on how technology has affected them.

THE NET GENERATION

Coomes and DeBard (2004) considered the Net Generation as a break from the previous Generation X; they described members of this generation as people who value authority, desire to be involved, and prefer to work in teams—all in drastic contrast to their immediate elders. Further, the Net Generation prefers conventionality and expects structure from the Baby Boomers, which is in direct contrast to Boomers and their predecessors. Howe and Strauss (2003) compared these young adults with the Silent Generation. The Silent Generation faced the Great Depression and World War II; their children emerged in a time of peace and prosperity: "No other adult peer group possesses anything close to [the Silent Generation's] upbeat, high-achieving, team-playing, and civic-minded reputation" (Howe & Strauss, 2003, p. 22). Because each new generation fills the social role of the eldest generation in society, Strauss and Howe (2006) expect that the Net Generation will replace the departing Silent Generation as the most optimistic and civic-minded generation in society.

The Net Generation is unique because of its members' comfort with technology. This is the most wired (technologically advanced) group of students ever to set foot on our campuses. Members of the Net Generation spend a great deal of time using technology in ways that members of other generations can only imagine, partly because of their early familiarity with technology: 20% of current college students began using computers between the ages of 5 and 8 years (Jones, 2002). In contrast, at the age of 5, their instructors may have been watching *The Six Million Dollar Man*, in which computers were large, room-sized machines with blinking lights. At that time (the 1970s), television writers were free to conjure up just about any fantastical vision of how computers might be used, because viewers were totally unfamiliar with such technology.

Net Generation students are tuned into the high-speed online world via high-bandwidth connections to the Internet. Thus, the culture of today's students self-propagates not only through the traditional methods of face-to-face interaction and media but also through the world of technology and the Internet. In fact, the market share of traditional media such as television, print newspapers, and radio has declined steadily since 2000 (see Project for Excellence in Journalism, 2006a; 2006b; 2006c), the year the Net Generation entered college. Net Generation students are comfortable using and testing bleeding-edge technology—technology that shows potential but has yet to demonstrate its value (Wikipedia, 2006).

CULTURE

Large cultural trends influence the values, beliefs, and attitudes of generations, as do historical events (Coomes, 2004). Society's influence has been even stronger on the Net Generation than on previous generations because its members have received targeted attention from marketing agencies since they were very young. While Gen Xers had *Sesame Street* to inform them as children, members of the Net Generation had many more sources of television influence, including traveling around the world with *Carmen Sandiego*, group living in *The Real World*, and programming from the Nickelodeon network. They have also been influenced by hip-hop culture (Coomes, 2004).

43

"Girl power" has been reinforced in the Net Generation's experience. Strong girls and women have appeared in television shows from *The Simpsons* (Lisa is the only reliable member of her family) to the *Powerpuff Girls, Buffy the Vampire Slayer*, *Alias*, and the *Gilmore Girls*. The entire concept of the *Gilmore Girls* is that a single mother and her daughter can not only survive on their own but can build happy and successful lives. Rory Gilmore is an outstanding high school student who moves on to Yale University; her mother, Lorelai, evolves from a teenage single mother to a businesswoman who owns an inn. Currently, more college undergraduates are female (57.6%) than male (National Center for Education Statistics, 2004).

TECHNOLOGY

In general, students from the Net Generation are familiar with and use technology more than those from previous generations. They are more likely to be online than people from other generations. In fact, there is almost an inverse relationship between age and Internet use: The younger people are, the more likely they are to be Internet users. The exception is Gen Xers, who use the Internet at rates identical to those of current 12–17-year-olds (87%; Fox & Madden, 2005). Fox and Madden (2005) found that 84% of Net Generation 18–28-year-olds are online, compared with 74% of Lead Boomers (aged 51–59 years) and 54% of the Silent Generation (aged 60–69 years). The Net Generation uses computers more than other generations. In a study of the first group of Net Generation students to arrive on college campuses, Sax, Ceja, and Teranishi (2001) found that 84.5% of first-year college students used computers frequently.

Net Generation students are avid users of the Internet for communication. Sax et al. (2001) reported that 64.1% of first-year college students frequently communicated via e-mail, and 70.2% frequently communicated via instant messaging. Recent data from a Pew Internet and American Life Project study showed that 66% and 75% of online 18–28-year-olds and 12–17-year-olds, respectively, use IM; while only 52%, 38%, and 33% of Gen Xers, Trail Boomers (aged 41–50 years), and the Silent Generation, respectively, use it (Fox & Madden, 2005). IM has become an easy way for Net Generation students to stay in touch with each other and keep their friends close, even when they go away to different colleges.

Social networking Web sites like MySpace and Facebook are popular among members of the Net Generation. Lenhart and Madden (2007) surveyed teenagers between the ages of 12 and 17 and found that 55% used a social networking site like MySpace or Facebook. Net Gen teens frequently visit these sites with 48% reporting that they log in daily or more often. Older (15-17 year old) teenage girls were more likely to use

44

social networking sites than older boys with 70% of girls reporting usage of a social networking site and only 57% of boys reporting online social networking. Net Generation teens use these sites to manage their real-life friendships—91% of social networking site users reported that they use the sites to stay in touch with current friends while only 49% reported using the sites to make new friends (Lenhart & Madden, 2007).

THE DIGITAL DIVIDE

Students from the Net Generation share cultural similarities even though they come from diverse cultural backgrounds. However, there are differences in technological skills among Net Generation students related to race, gender, class, and academic background (See Table 3.1 for a comprehensive summary). Sax et al. (2001) studied 272,821 first-year college students and found that, even after controlling for income levels, Latinos and African Americans were less likely than Whites and Asian Americans to communicate via e-mail. Even at early ages, differences in computer use exist. In a study of 1,065 parents of children between the ages of 6 months and 6 years, Calvert, Rideout, Woolard, Barr, and Strouse (2005) found that children from Latino families were less likely to use computers than children from White families.

45

Differences in the use of technology can be understood by looking at access for different ethnic and socioeconomic groups. In a nationwide study using census data, the Department of Commerce National Telecommunications and Information Administration (NTIA, 2004) found that only 37.2% of Latinos and 45.6% of African Americans used the Internet, compared with 65.1% of Whites and 63.1% of Asian Americans. Furthermore, only 12.6% of Latinos and 14.2% of African Americans lived in households with broadband Internet access, compared with 25.7% of Whites and 34.2% of Asian Americans. The NTIA study also found that Internet use and access to broadband at home is a linear function of income—people with lower incomes have lower rates of Internet use and broadband access. These findings were replicated in Pew Internet and American Life Project surveys, which found that households earning $75,000 or more per year have broadband access and use the Internet at rates almost three times those of people at the lowest socioeconomic level (Horrigan, 2006; Horrigan & Rainie, 2005).

Differences also exist in *how* people from lower socioeconomic levels use computers. Children from lower socioeconomic areas are more likely to have their learning "led" by computer than those from higher socioeconomic areas, who are more likely to learn how to *control* the computer. Brown, Higgins, and Hartley (2001); Milone and Salpeter (1996); Pisapia (1994); and Warschauer, Knobel, and Stone (2004) found that students in public schools in lower socioeconomic areas were more likely to use computers for academic practice and quizzing, while students in higher socioeconomic areas were more than three times as likely to be learning how to program computers. While gaps in access to computers have narrowed between students in low and high socioeconomic areas, students in high socioeconomic areas are more likely than those in lower socioeconomic areas to use computers to carry out research, create projects and demonstrations, and analyze data. Furthermore, teachers in lower socioeconomic areas significantly underestimate the percentage of their students who have computers at home (they believe that around 50% have computers; 84% do); therefore, they tend not to assign computer-based homework (Warschauer et al., 2004).

Researchers have also found gender differences in the use of the Internet and computers. Fallows (2005) found that even though women are catching up to men in terms of being online, their use of the Internet lags slightly: 68% of men and 66% of women use the Internet. Interestingly, younger women (86% of women ages 18–29 years) are more likely to be online than younger men (80% of men ages 18–29 years). Men use the Internet for a wider variety of tasks than women do—women tend to use it for communication and connection, while men tend to use it for entertainment and research (Fallows, 2005). ClickZ Stats (2002), citing Nielsen NetRatings data, states that men log on to the Internet more, spend more time online, and access more content than women. Male students have reported that they find it easier to address emotional issues when using the Internet to communicate and may use the medium as a buffer to negotiate difficult emotional states (Junco, 2005).

There are clear differences related to educational attainment in the use of the Internet and broadband access. As with socioeconomic status, the pattern is linear: People with less education are less likely to use the Internet and to have broadband access at home. A person with less than a high school education is two to six times less likely to be an Internet user and three to six times less likely to have broadband access at home than a person with a college education (Horrigan, 2006; NTIA, 2004; Horrigan & Rainie, 2005).

Table 3.1 summarizes the findings of five studies of Internet accessibility; the results are broken down by gender, age, race, and socioeconomic status. Some of the findings are quite different; for instance, in one of the Pew Project studies, Horrigan (2006) found that 41% of Latinos live in homes with broadband access, while the NTIA study (2004) found that only 12.6% of Latinos had such access. It is important to note that the Horrigan (2006) study is more recent than the NTIA study and that Horrigan (2006) found a large percentage increase in broadband access across all groups between 2005 and 2006. On the other hand, because it used census data, the NTIA study (2004) sample was more than 20 times larger than the largest of the Pew samples.

While there may be important implications for the increases in broadband access for persons from minority backgrounds found in the Pew samples, it is too early to make valid inferences. The Pew data are much newer and could indicate actual increases in the percentages of Latinos and African Americans who have broadband access at home. This may be due to an increase in broadband coverage and a decrease in cost. This hypothesis is supported by the fact that persons from urban areas are more likely than those from rural areas to cite expense as a prohibitive factor in having broadband access at home (NTIA, 2004). The cost for DSL broadband access has continued to decrease; it dropped 8% between February 2004 and December 2005 (Horrigan, 2006).

Another possible explanation for the discrepancies between the Pew and NTIA data lies in how the data are collected and analyzed. The NTIA sample is more representative of the overall U.S. population because it uses U.S. Census data. The U.S. Census collects information through mailed surveys and follows up with telephone calls and personal visits to those who do not return their surveys (U.S. Census Bureau, 2002). The Pew studies rely on phone interviewing, a technique that can often result in poor response rates, which leads Pew to compensate by weighing its data along demographic lines using a formula derived from U.S. Census information. The response rate percentages for the Pew interviews average in the mid- to high-20s, while the overall response rate for the 2000 Census was 67% (U.S. Census Bureau, 2005). The statistics for Latino respondents may be further skewed in the Pew data because Pew conducts its interviews only in English, while the U.S. Census uses report forms in multiple languages.

Table 3.1 shows some of the findings of the more comprehensive studies of Internet use and broadband access of the U.S. population. The Pew Internet and American Life Project's report *Home Broadband Adoption 2006* (Horrigan, 2006) was based on a sample of 4,001 adults surveyed in 2006. The Pew memo "Generations Online" (Fox & Madden, 2005) included samples of 6,403 adults and 1,100 teens who were surveyed via phone interviews in 2004 and 2005. The Pew report *How Women and Men Use the Internet* (Fallows, 2005) included 6,403 respondents polled in 2005. The Rainie and Horrigan (2005) Pew Research Center report *A Decade of Adoption: How the Internet Has Woven Itself Into American Life* included 2,200 adult respondents polled in 2004. The NTIA report *A Nation Online: Entering the Broadband Age* (2004) is based on the U.S. Census Bureau's 2003 survey of 57,000 households containing 134,000 persons.

Table 3.1. **Summary of four comprehensive studies of Internet use and broadband access.**

	NTIA: *A Nation Online*[5]		Pew Internet and American Life Project reports/memos	
Gender				
	Women	59.2%	Women	66%[3]
	Men	58.2%	Men	68%
Ethnicity				
	Latino	37.2%	Latino	59%[4]
	African Amer.	45.6%	African Amer.	43%
	Asian Amer.	63.1%	White	67%
	White	65.1%		
Age				
	10–13	67.3%	12–17	87%[2]
	14–17	78.8%	18–24	82%
	18–24	70.6%	25–29	85%
	25–49	68.0%	30–34	83%
	50+	44.8%	35–39	80%
			40–44	76%
			45–49	73%
			50–54	68%
			55–59	68%
			60–64	55%
Family Income				
	<$15,000	31.2%	<$30,000	44%[4]
	15,000–24,999	38.0%	30,000–50,000	69%
	25,000–34,999	48.9%	50,000–75,000	81%
	35,000–49,999	62.1%	75,000+	89%
	50,000–74,999	71.8%		
	75,000+	82.9%		
Educational Attainment				
	<High School	15.5%	<High School	32%[4]
	High School	44.5%	High School	52%
	Some College	68.6%	Some College	75%
	Bachelor's	84.9%	College +	88%
	Bachelor's +	88.0%		

(Internet users)

49

	NTIA: *A Nation Online*[5]		Pew Internet and American Life Project reports/memos	
Lives in broadband household	**Gender**			
	Women	21.8%	Women	38%[1]
	Men	23.9%	Men	45%
	Ethnicity			
	Latino	12.6%	Latino	41%[1]
	African Amer.	14.2%	African Amer.	31%
	Asian Amer.	34.2%	White	42%
	White	25.7%		
	Age			
	10–13	25.8%	12–17	49%[2]
	14–17	28.3%	18–24	40%
	18–24	25.5%	25–29	40%
	25–49	25.9%	30–34	42%
	50+	15.9%	35–39	36%
			40–44	35%
			45–49	36%
			50–54	32%
			55–59	27%
			60–64	23%
	Family Income			
	<$15,000	7.5%	<$30,000	21%[1]
	15,000–24,999	9.3%	30,000–50,000	43%
	25,000–34,999	13.4%	50,000–75,000	48%
	35,000–49,999	19.0%	75,000+	68%
	50,000–74,999	27.9%		
	75,000+	45.4%		
	Educational Attainment			
	<High School	5.9%	<High School	17%[1]
	High School	14.5%	High School	31%
	Some College	23.7%	Some College	47%
	Bachelor's	34.9%	College +	62%
	Bachelor's +	38.0%		

[1]Pew Internet and American Life Project report Home Broadband Adoption 2006 (Horrigan 2006). N=4,001. Survey conducted in 2006.
[2]Pew Internet and American Life Project data memo "Generations Online" (Fox & Madden, 2005). N =6,403 adults and 1,100 teens. Survey conducted in 2004–05.
[3]Pew Internet and American Life Project report How Women and Men Use the Internet (Fallows, 2005). N=6,403. Survey conducted in 2005.
[4]Pew Internet and American Life Project report A Decade of Adoption: How the Internet Has Woven Itself Into American Life (Rainie & Horrigan, 2005). N=2,200 adults. Survey conducted in 2004.
[5]U. S. Department of Commerce National Telecommunications and Information Administration report A Nation Online: Entering the Broadband Age (2004). N=134,000 persons ages 3 years and older. Survey conducted in 2003.

NET GENERATION STUDENTS

Net Generation college students use computers and technology differently and at higher rates than students from other generations and people who are not in college. For the Pew Internet and American Life Project report *The Internet Goes to College: How Students Are Living in the Future With Today's Technology* (Jones, 2002), researchers asked college students about their use of technology. The report stated that

- 86% of college students had been online, compared with 59% of all Americans

- 72% of college students checked their e-mail daily, while only 52% of all Americans with Internet access did so

- 78% of college Internet users went online to browse for fun, compared with 64% of all Internet users

- 60% of college Internet users had downloaded files online, compared with 28% of all Internet users

- 26% of college students used instant messaging on an average day, compared with 12% of all Internet users

The same study asked students about the impact of the Internet on their academics and communication, and reported that:

- 79% of students said that using the Internet had a positive impact on their academics

- 46% of students said e-mail allows them to express ideas to professors that they would not express in person

- 42% of students use the Internet most often to communicate socially; almost an equal number (38%) use the Internet to do classwork

51

Impact of Technology

Academics

There are conflicting reports about how the Internet has affected Net Generation students. The Internet may have a positive effect on students' interactions with each other and with faculty members. For instance, Hu and Kuh (2001) examined the responses of 18,844 college students at 71 institutions on the College Student Experiences Questionnaire (CSEQ). They found that attending a "wired" campus (that is, one with readily available Internet technology, as defined by the Yahoo! Internet Life survey of wired campuses) was positively related to students reporting good educational practices (student/faculty contact, cooperation among students, and active learning). While some may think wired campuses decrease personal interactions, Hu and Kuh (2001) found that students at wired institutions reported *more* contact with their professors and *more* peer interactions.

Supporting the Hu and Kuh (2001) findings, a Pew Internet and American Life Project survey (Jones, 2002) found that Net Generation students reported positive outcomes as a result of Internet use. Almost 79% of students reported that the Internet had a positive impact on their academics, and most students reported that relationships with their professors had been positively affected by Internet and e-mail communication. Students reported using e-mail to discuss grades, set up appointments, and get clarification on assignments. In this survey, 46% of students reported that e-mail allowed them to express ideas to professors that they would not have expressed in class.

In another study using the CSEQ, Kuh and Vesper (2001) found that even when background characteristics and academic ability were taken into account, students who learned more about computers during college reported higher gains in skills considered essential for success in college than those who learned less about computers. The improvement in skills included gains in the ability to think analytically, to learn on one's own, and to understand oneself, as well as awareness of other philosophies. Kuh and Vesper (2001) also found that those who reported higher gains in computer skills spent more time studying than those who reported lower gains.

Social Interaction and Communication

Research supports the idea that the Internet (specifically, chat applications such as IM) enhances Net Generation students' social skills and psychological well-being. Campbell, Cumming, and Hughes (2006) found that undergraduate student chat users were less likely to report being socially fearful than non-chat users. The researchers asserted that the Internet is a low-risk method of learning about social interactions. These findings support a study by Shaw and Gant (2002) in which college students engaged in five sequential anonymous chats about low-risk topics; the students were assessed before, during, and after the chats using a number of psychosocial inventories (the Center for Epidemiological Studies Depression Scale, the Revised UCLA Loneliness Scale, the Texas Social Behavior Inventory, and the Cohen-Hoberman Interpersonal Support Evaluation List). Shaw and Gant (2002) found that between the first and last assessments, the students' scores on scales measuring negative effects (depression and loneliness) decreased significantly and their scores on scales measuring positive effects (social support and self-esteem) increased significantly.

53

On the other hand, some researchers believe that the Internet may negatively affect Net Generation college students' academic progress as well as their interactions with each other and with faculty members. Kubey, Lavin, and Barrows (2001) conducted a survey of 576 mostly first-year students and found that 9% agreed or strongly agreed that they might be "a little psychologically dependent on the Internet." The students in the dependent group were significantly more likely than those in the non-dependent group to agree or strongly agree that if they had a few more friends, they would probably use the Internet less. The Internet-dependent group included a disproportionate number of first-year students, and they felt significantly more alone than other students.

In the same survey, 14% of the respondents reported that their schoolwork had been hurt occasionally, frequently, or very frequently by Internet use. Compared with the nondependent group, four times as many students in the Internet-dependent group reported Internet-related academic impairment. Additionally, the group of students who reported that their schoolwork had been hurt by Internet use reported that they used the Internet at rates more than double that of the sample as a whole. The students who reported academic impairment because of the Internet were significantly more likely than those in the nonimpaired group to agree or strongly agree that if they had a few more friends, they would probably use the Internet less. The group reporting academic impairment included a disproportionate number of first-year students (Kubey, Lavin, & Barrows, 2001). These findings suggest that Net Generation students, especially first-year students, may be at risk of developing academic difficulties because of Internet use.

An important consideration in conceptualizing Net Generation student computer use is the impact technology has on student academic performance. Morgan and Cotten (2003) found that first-year students spent an average of 16.3 hours a week chatting and using IM, and an average of 3.9 hours a week using e-mail. The Pew Internet and American Life Project found that 83% of those in the Net Generation use IM, and over 57% use it more frequently than e-mail (Shiu & Lenhart, 2004). Finally, Mastrodicasa and Kepic (2005) found that more than half of the students at a large southeastern university check their university e-mail accounts multiple times a day, and 29% of students check e-mail between two and six days a week. Furthermore, the Pew Internet and American Life Project report *The Internet Goes to College* (Jones, 2002) reported that 62% of students study no more than seven hours a week, and the Cooperative Institutional Research Program of the Higher Education Research Institute (Pryor, Hurtado, Saenz, Lindholm, Korn, & Mahoney, 2005) reported that only 32% of first-year college students spent six or more hours a week studying during their last year in high school. A pattern begins to emerge when combining these data: Net Generation students spend much more time communicating via IM than doing even the minimum recommended amount of schoolwork.

The data show that Net Generation college students prefer IM to other forms of electronic communication such as e-mail. IM allows students to address emotional issues and make frank or unpleasant statements without having to deal with others in person. While this may seem like an inappropriate shield from real-life interpersonal interactions, some research suggests that communicating via IM is helpful for some students, especially those who are introverted or feel awkward in social situations. Koch and Pratarelli (2004) found that introverts reported a strong preference for online communication over face-to-face interactions. Introverted students reported being happiest when using their computers and reported significantly more ease in talking with people on the Internet, having more fun with people on the Internet than in person, and preferring to spend their evenings online.

55

These findings and conclusions were echoed by Junco (2005), who found that many students preferred using IM to dealing in person with emotionally charged issues. In interviews conducted by Junco (2005) asking students about how they've used IM to deal with difficult interpersonal situations, student comments included:

☞ "It's easier to say things over IM, because you can't see their facial expressions, which could upset you."

☞ "I told [my boyfriend] it was over...I used e-mail and IM because it was easier. I knew if I did it in person it would be 10 times more emotional and I would cry, and I didn't want to give him that satisfaction" (p. 231).

☞ "It's easy because you don't really know what the person is thinking. Face to face, you know what they think; on IM, you can say what you want and you won't see the emotions or the tears."

☞ "For some people, it's easier for them to message someone. Like if you really have feelings for someone and can't express it in person, instant messaging makes it easier to talk to that person and get everything out."

☞ "I said let's talk on here (IM).... I didn't want this guy to see my face, to see my emotion and how he made me feel. So I only agreed to talk to him on IM."

Psychological Effects

Kubey et al. (2001) and others (Chou, Condron, & Belland, 2005; Engelberg & Sjöberg, 2004) have described the negative psychological and academic effects of Internet dependence or addiction. Other researchers have investigated this phenomenon and reported both positive and negative effects. In one study, Morgan and Cotten (2003), using a sample of 287 first-year college students, found that increased e-mail and IM hours were associated with decreased depressive symptoms (as measured by the Center for Epidemiologic Studies Depression Scale–Iowa Version), while increased Internet hours for shopping, research, or playing games were associated with increased depressive symptoms. In other words, using the Internet for interpersonal connection promotes psychological well-being. Morgan and Cotten found that increased e-mail and IM hours yielded a larger decrease in depressive symptoms for men than for women.

56

Summary

Whether the Internet negatively or positively affects students' psychosocial and academic development will be a subject for research and debate for years to come. One thing is certain: Net Generation students use the Internet to communicate, and they maintain a close group of friends through IM, social networking Web sites, chat, and e-mail. Additionally, most Net Generation college students maintain relationships with a group of high school friends through the Internet, which is markedly different from previous generations of college students who tended to create a social network with their new college friends and to communicate less with high school friends (Kubey et al., 2001). In addition to maintaining high school friendships, Net Generation students keep in touch with their families in ways that they might not have done before the advent of the Internet.

Recommendations

☞ As the technology used by Net Generation students changes and develops rapidly, faculty and student affairs professionals must keep up with current research. This book takes the first step by outlining some of the broad issues facing those who work with the Net Generation. Because of the speed of change, some of the material will be dated by the time this book is published. Higher education professionals who work with Net Generation students should have a personal professional development plan to make sure they are aware of the latest research trends.

☞ Administrators must take the digital divide into account in their institutional plans. They must ensure that students who are not as familiar with technology are helped to bring their skills up to speed. If the institution requires students to possess specific technology (e.g., a laptop), the institution must have a process through which students who may not be able to afford the technology can acquire it.

☞ It is important to identify students who are inclined to have psychosocial problems because of their Internet use (for instance, students who use the Internet primarily for noncommunication purposes) and to create interventions to help them. Conversely, it is important to encourage students in the positive use of technology (for example, engaging in online chats with their classmates and their professors about course material).

REFERENCES

Brown, M., Higgins, K., & Hartley, K. (2001). Teachers and technology equity. *Teaching Exceptional Children, 33*(4), 32–39.

Calvert, S. L., Rideout, V. J., Woolard, J. L., Barr, R. F., & Strouse, G. A. (2005). Age, ethnicity, and socioeconomic patterns in early computer use. *American Behavioral Scientist, 48*(5), 590–607.

Campbell, A. J., Cumming, S. R., & Hughes, I. (2006). Internet use by the socially fearful: Addiction or therapy? *Cyberpsychology and Behavior 9*(1), 69–81.

Chou, C., Condron, L., & Belland, J. C. (2005). A review of the research on Internet addiction. *Educational Psychology Review, 17*(4), 363–388.

ClickZ Stats. (2002, January). Men still dominate worldwide Internet usage. Retrieved September 26, 2006, from http://www.clickz.com/stats/demographics/article.php/959421

Coomes, M. D. (2004). Understanding the historical and cultural influences that shape generations. In M. D. Coomes & R. DeBard (Eds.), *Serving the millennial generation: New directions for student services, no. 106* (pp. 17–31). San Francisco: Jossey-Bass.

Coomes, M. D., & DeBard, R. (2004). A generational approach to understanding students. In M. D. Coomes & R. DeBard (Eds.), *Serving the millennial generation: New directions for student services, no. 106* (pp. 5–16). San Francisco: Jossey-Bass.

Engleberg, E. & Sjöberg, L. (2004). Internet use, social skills, and adjustment. *Cyberpsychology and Behavior 7*(1), 41–47.

Fallows, D. (2005). *How women and men use the Internet*. Washington, DC: Pew Internet and American Life Project.

Fox, S., & Madden, M. (2005, December). Generations online. Data memo posted to Pew Internet and American Life Project Web site, Retrieved

September 25, 2006, from http://www.pewinternet.org/pdfs/PIP_Generations_Memo.pdf

Horrigan, J. B. (2006). *Home broadband adoption 2006*. Washington, DC: Pew Internet and American Life Project.

Horrigan, J., & Rainie, L. (2005). Internet: The Mainstreaming of Online Life. *Trends*, Pew Research Center. Retrieved January 30, 2007, from http://www.pewinternet.org/report_display.asp?r=148, January 30, 2007.

Howe, N., & Strauss, W. (2003). *Millennials go to college – strategies for a new generation on campus: Recruiting and admissions, campus life, and the classroom*. Great Falls, VA: American Association of Registrars and Admissions Officers and LifeCourse Associates.

Hu, S., & Kuh, G. D. (2001). Computing experience and good practices in undergraduate education: Does the degree of campus "wiredness" matter? *Education Policy Analysis Archives, 9*(49). Retrieved September 26, 2006, from http://epaa.asu.edu/epaa/v9n49.html

Jones, S. (2002). *The Internet goes to college: How students are living in the future with today's technology.* Washington, DC: Pew Internet and American Life Project.

Junco, R. (2005). Technology and today's first-year students. In M. L. Upcraft, J. N. Gardner, B. O. Barefoot, & associates (Eds.), *Meeting challenges and building support: Creating a climate for first-year student success* (pp. 221–238). San Francisco: Jossey-Bass.

Koch, W. H., & Pratarelli, M. E. (2004). Effects of intro-/extraversion and sex on social Internet use. *North American Journal of Psychology, 6*(3), 371–382.

Kubey, R. W., Lavin, M. J., & Barrows, J. R. (2001). Internet use and collegiate academic performance decrements: Early findings. *Journal of Communication, 51*, 366–382.

Kuh, G. D., & Vesper, N. (2001). Do computers enhance or detract from student learning? *Research in Higher Education, 42*(1), 87–102.

Lenhart, A., & Madden, M. (2007, January). Social networking websites and teens: An overview. Data memo posted to Pew Internet and American Life Project Web site, Retrieved January 25, 2007, from http://www.pewinternet.org/pdfs/PIP_SNS_Data_Memo_Jan_2007.pdf

Mastrodicasa, J. M., & Kepic, G. (2005). *Parents gone wild.* Paper presented at the national meeting of the National Academic Advising Association, Las Vegas, NV.

Milone, M. N., & Salpeter, J. (1996). Technology and equity issues. *Technology & Learning, 16*(4), 38–47.

Morgan, C., & Cotten, S. R. (2003). The relationship between Internet activities and depressive symptoms in a sample of college freshmen. *Cyberpsychology and Behavior, 6*(2), 133–142.

National Center for Education Statistics (NCES). (2004). Undergraduate data—all postsecondary students. Retrieved November 10, 2006, from http://nces.ed.gov/dasol/tables/#pse_students

Pisapia, J. (1994). *Technology: The equity issue.* Research Brief No.14. Richmond, VA: Metropolitan Educational Research Consortium.

Prensky, M. (2001). Digital natives, digital immigrants, part II: Do they really think differently? *On the Horizon 9*(6), 1–9.

Project for Excellence in Journalism. (2006a). *The state of the news media 2006: An annual report on American journalism: Network TV.* Retrieved October 30, 2006, from http://www.stateofthenewsmedia.org/2006/narrative_networktv_audience.asp?cat=3&media=5

Project for Excellence in Journalism. (2006b). *The state of the news media 2006: An annual report on American journalism: Radio.* Retrieved October 30, 2006, from http://www.stateofthenewsmedia.org/2006/narrative_radio_audience.asp?cat=3&media=9

Project for Excellence in Journalism. (2006c). *The state of the news media 2006: An annual report on American journalism: Newspapers.* Retrieved October 30, 2006, from http://www.stateofthenewsmedia.org/2006/narrative_newspapers_audience.asp?cat=3&media=3

Pryor, J. H., Hurtado, S., Saenz, V. B., Lindholm, J. A., Korn, W. S., & Mahoney, K. M. (2005). *The American freshman: National norms for fall 2005.* Los Angeles, CA: Cooperative Institutional Research Program: Higher Education Research Institute, University of California, Los Angeles.

Rainie, L., & Horrigan, J. (2005). *A decade of adoption: How the Internet has woven itself into American life.* Washington, DC: Pew Internet and American Life Project.

Sax, L. J., Ceja, M., & Teranishi, R. T. (2001). Technological preparedness among entering freshmen: The role of race, class, and gender. *Journal of Educational Computing Research, 24*(4), 363–383.

Shaw, L. H., & Gant, L. M. (2002). In defense of the Internet: The relationship between Internet communication and depression, loneliness, self-esteem, and perceived social support. *Cyberpsychology and Behavior (5)*2, 157–171.

Shiu, E., & Lenhart, A. (2004). *How Americans use instant messaging.* Washington, DC: Pew Internet and American Life Project.

Strauss, W., & Howe, N. (2006). *Millennials and the pop culture: Strategies for a new generation of consumers in music, movies, television, the Internet, and video games.* Great Falls, VA: LifeCourse Associates.

Strauss, W., & Howe, N. (1991). *Generations: The history of America's future, 1584-2069.* New York: Morrow.

United States Census Bureau. (2002). *Census 2000 basics.* Washington, DC: Author.

United States Census Bureau. (2005). Census 2000 final response rates.

Retrieved September 26, 2006, from http://www.census.gov/dmd/www/response/2000response.html

United States Department of Commerce National Telecommunications and Information Administration (NTIA). (2004). A nation online: Entering the broadband age. Retrieved September 26, 2006, from http://www.ntia.doc.gov/reports/anol/NationOnlineBroadband04.htm

Warschauer, M., Knobel, M., & Stone, L. (2004). Technology and equity in schooling: Deconstructing the digital divide. *Educational Policy,* 18(4), 562–588.

Wikipedia. (2006). *Bleeding edge*. Retrieved September 26, 2006, from http://en.wikipedia.org/wiki/Bleeding_edge

Chapter 4

Net Generation Survey Results

College students from the Net Generation are often misunderstood by individuals from other generations—a common problem when interpreting the norms of one cultural group through the lens of another. For instance, Generation Xers, Boomers, and members of the Silent Generation are often very surprised to know that Net Generation students welcome "helicopter parenting"; and student affairs professionals frequently comment on how the Net Generation uses technology much more and in different ways than generations before them. Surprisingly, though, not much research is available on what these students are actually doing with technology and how their interactions with their parents work. On these topics, information about the Net Generation is often speculation or based on studies with limited sample sizes.

This chapter introduces the Net Generation Survey and summarizes survey data aimed at understanding the Net Generation's use of technology. The survey sample includes students at seven institutions and is part of an ongoing effort to assess and understand the experiences of Net Generation students. We created the survey to gauge current student online activities, access to technology, and communication with parents.

SURVEY DEVELOPMENT

We used a multi-step process to create the survey. First, we collated all the data we had collected over the past three years from focus groups and student interviews. Then we reviewed the Pew Internet and American Life Project surveys as well as Mastrodicasa and Kepic's (2005) survey. We selected questions on the basis of what we wanted to know about the Net Generation. These questions covered their use of cellular phones, Facebook, MySpace, and blogs, as well as information about communication with parents. Finally, we asked two groups of Net Generation students to review the survey and provide feedback. We used the feedback to refine the survey, and then pilot tested it with a different group of students. After the pilot test, we revised the survey and sent it to colleagues for feedback. We incorporated their feedback into the final version of the Net Generation Survey.

SURVEY ADMINISTRATION

The survey was hosted on SurveyMonkey.com, a commercial survey Web site. SurveyMonkey allows users to create, edit, and distribute surveys from a Web-based portal. Links to the survey were sent via e-mail to all of the enrolled students at seven institutions (N=88,612) during the spring and fall 2006 semesters. There were 7,705 responses—an overall response rate of 8.7%. For individual institution sizes, responses, and responses rates, see Table 4.1. At first, the overall response rate seemed low; however, further investigation revealed a pattern. The smaller institutions in the sample had better response rates than the larger institutions (the response rates for institutions larger than 15,000 students was 7.1% while the rate was 16.2% for those smaller than 15,000). There are four possible explanations, either alone or in combination, for the low response rates:

1. No incentives were offered for completing the survey. Students at larger institutions are bombarded with invitations to participate in surveys, and many include incentives. A colleague at one of the larger institutions in the sample told us that another online survey administered at the same time as the Net Generation Survey offered $500 incentives, through a drawing, to a lucky few students.

2. As reported by colleagues at various institutions and by Carnevale (2006), Net Gen students are less and less likely to access their institutionally provided e-mail accounts. One colleague at an institution that participated in the survey reported that roughly 10% of e-mails sent for research requests are returned as undeliverable because the students' inboxes are full, presumably because they never check their institutional e-mail accounts.

3. Net Generation students are very aware of spam and phishing scams (e-mail scams in which the sender tries to trick the recipient into divulging confidential information—such as the password to an online banking site). Some students consider all e-mails from their institu-

67

tions to be spam and delete them without reading them (Carnevale, 2006). The authors received a number of e-mails from students asking whether our survey was "legit"; some students said they originally thought it was a phishing scam. Students may have been suspicious or uninterested enough to delete the e-mail message without reading it.

4. The Net Generation Survey, because it is the first of its kind, asks a broad range of questions about technology use. The survey is admittedly long for Net Generation students' attention spans. As mentioned in chapter 3, these students are avid multitaskers, with shorter attention spans than persons from other generations. A long survey such as this one may have deterred students who would have participated if it had been shorter.

Table 4.1. **Net Generation Survey: Institution sizes, responses, and response rates.**

Institution Size	Responses	Response Rate
21,538	706	3.3%
21,132	1,733	8.2%
15,540	817	5.3%
15,000	1,956	13%
5,400	597	11%
5,300	1,492	28.2%
4,702	404	8.6%

RESULTS

Demographics

Results for the demographic survey items are shown in Table 4.2: 5.6% of students reported being from a Latino background, 6.2% from an African American background, 3.1% from an Asian American background, 0.6% from a Native American background, and 78.3% from a white background. The sample was predominantly female, with 62.4% women and 37.6% men. Most survey respondents were traditional-aged college students—77.6% were between the ages of 18 and 23 years. Female Net Generations students were more likely to respond to the survey. This could be due to the fact that women use the Internet more for communication than men and therefore, check and respond to e-mail more often (Fallows, 2005; Junco, 2005).

Table 4.2. Net Generation Survey: Demographic data (N=7,705).

Gender	
Women	62.4%
Men	37.6%
Ethnicity	
White	78.3%
African American	6.2%
Latino	5.6%
Asian American	3.1%
Native American	0.6%
Other	6.2%
Age	
18	14.4%
19	17.1%
20	15.9%
21	14.3%
22	10.3%

23	5.6%
24	3.9%
25	2.8%
26	2.2%
27	1.4%
28	1.5%
29	1.2%
30	1.1
31–63	<0.9% each
Family Income	
<$9,999	2.3%
10,000–14,999	2.1%
15,000–24,999	3.7%
25,000–34,999	5.9%
35,000–49,999	10.4%
50,000–74,999	17.4%
75,000–99,999	12.7%
100,000–149,999	12.0%
150,000–199,999	4.2%
>$200,000	4.3%
Don't Know	25.0%
Parent Educational Attainment	
<High School	4.1%
High School Graduate	24.4%
Some College	22.7%
College Graduate	33.7%
Completed Graduate School	15.0%
Class Standing	
First Year/Freshman	22.2%
Sophomore	16.4%
Junior	23.0%
Senior	27.6%
Graduate Student	10.8%
Technology Ownership	
Computer	97.3%
Cell Phone	94.1%
MP3 Player	56.4%

COMMUNICATION WITH PARENTS

Net Generation students reported speaking with their parents an average of over one-and-a-half times a day, with students initiating the calls 57.6% of the time (n=6,667). The frequency of Net Gen students' conversations with their parents while the parents are at work, driving their cars, or at home is shown in Figure 4.1. Most of the time Net Generation students are speaking with their parents, the parents are at home; however, many conversations occur while the parents are at work or driving in their cars. Figure 4.2 shows the most frequent topics in conversations with parents.

Figure 4.1. Net Generation Survey: Frequency of students' conversations with their parents when parents are at work, in the car, and at home (n=6,869).

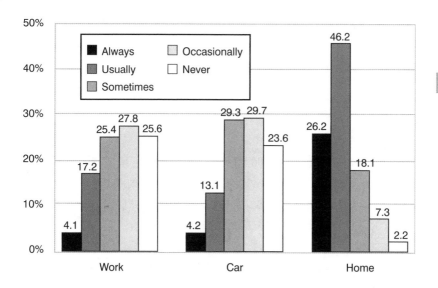

Figure 4.2. **Net Generation Survey: Reported conversation topics when students speak with their parents (n=6,869).**

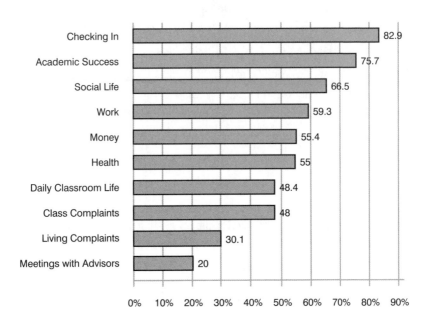

USE OF INSTANT MESSAGING

A full 75.5% of our sample (n=5,184) use some type of instant messaging program. AOL Instant Messenger is the preferred software; MSN Messenger is the next most popular; and Yahoo! Messenger is third. Students reported being logged on to IM programs a median of 35 hours each week. The largest proportion of IM users (15%) is logged on 24 hours a day, 7 days a week. IM users reported that they actively chat 80 minutes each day (median). Figure 4.3 shows the distribution of the time students spend chatting each day. Just over 18.5% of the sample also use IM on their wireless devices (cell phones, PDAs, etc.). Finally, 79.7% of IM users send IMs to people who are in the same physical location (such as a residence hall room or apartment). Figure 4.4 shows the percentage of IM users who included various types of information in their IM profiles or their away messages. As can be seen from the chart, inspirational or funny quotations are most likely to be included in IM profiles or away messages.

Figure 4.3. **Net Generation Survey: Distribution of the time IM users spend chatting on IM each day (n=4,801).**

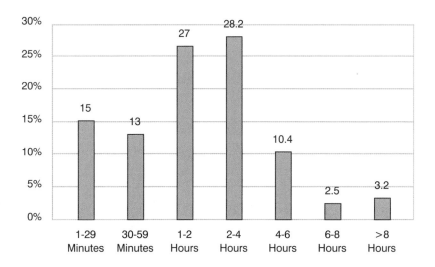

Figure 4.4. Net Generation Survey: Percentage of IM users who included contact information, inspirational or funny quotations, Web links, links to online photo albums, personal news, gossip, or location on their instant message profiles or away messages (n=5,184).

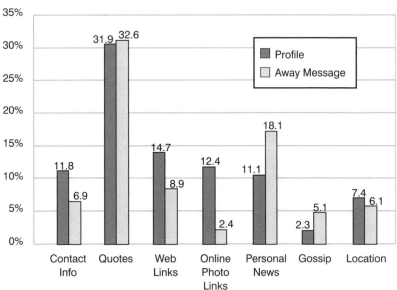

Multitasking

Net Generation students are avid multitaskers—they perform a number of tasks simultaneously that require cognitive resources and attention. Of all IM users (n=5,184), 91.9% reported doing something else on the computer at the same time, while 75.1% reported engaging in non-computer-related activities (such as watching TV or talking on the phone) frequently while IMing. Figure 4.5 shows the frequency with which Net Gen students reported using IM and doing schoolwork at the same time: 75% of IM users reported using IM and doing schoolwork simultaneously.

In addition to questions about multitasking, the Net Generation Survey included a question about how online activities impacted student academics. Figure 4.6 shows how frequently Net Gen students' schoolwork had been hurt because they played video games, used IM, or surfed the Web. A sizeable proportion of IM users reported that their schoolwork was hurt "more than sometimes" by surfing the Web (40.2%), by IM use (28%) and by playing games (16.3%).

Figure 4.5. Net Generation Survey: Reported frequency of multitasking by using IM and performing schoolwork at the same time (n=5,184).

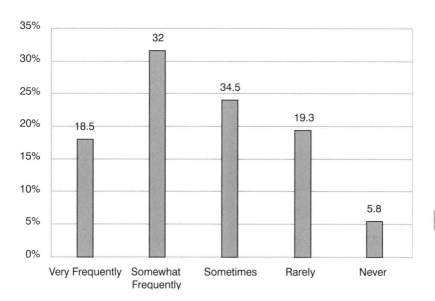

75

Figure 4.6. Net Generation Survey: How frequently playing games, using IM, or surfing the Web hurt schoolwork (n=5,184).

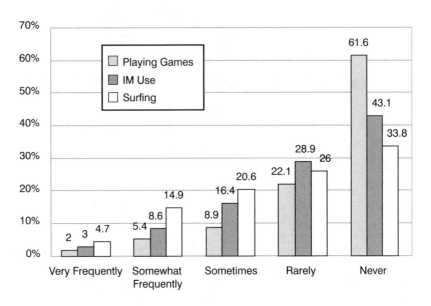

INFORMATION STREAMING

Through focus groups and interviews conducted before the survey, the authors determined that many Net Generation students get news through formats that are very different from those other generations used. The data supported this observation. As shown in Table 4.3, an almost equal proportion of Net Generation students obtained news via television and online (n=6,566). Figures 4.7 and 4.8 list the TV shows and Web sites that students primarily use to obtain news. There was great variability in the "Other" category for news Web sites; one possible reason is that students who get their news from the Web may be more inclined to seek out alternative sources of news.

Table 4.3. Net Generation Survey: Primary sources students use to get news (n=6,566).

News Source	Percentage
Television	39.7
Web sites	33.7
Newspaper	11.1
Radio	7.5
Other	5.9
Online video streaming	.9
Blog	.7
Online audio streaming	.4

Figure 4.7. Net Generation Survey: Percentage of respondents who watch specific news programs or networks (of those respondents who use television as their primary source for news; n=2,606).

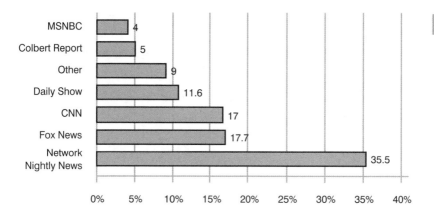

Figure 4.8. Net Generation Survey: Percentage of respondents who use specific Web sites to get news (of those respondents who use the Web as their primary source to obtain news; n=2,213).

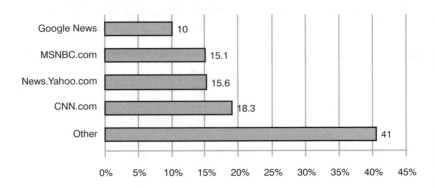

Blogs

Blogs have grown rapidly in popularity over the past few years, and Net Generation students have embraced them: 27.9% report that they have blogs (n=1,830). In contrast, in a recent Pew Internet and American Life Project survey (Lenhart & Madden, 2005) only 7% of all adults reported having a blog. The 44.4% of Net Generation students who reported reading blogs typically read them an hour (median) a week (n=2,914). Figure 4.9 shows the Web sites the bloggers in the sample used to host blogs.

Figure 4.9. Net Generation Survey: Blog-hosting sites used by respondents who reported having a blog. (Percentages do not add up to 100 because bloggers sometimes have more than one blog; n=1,830.)

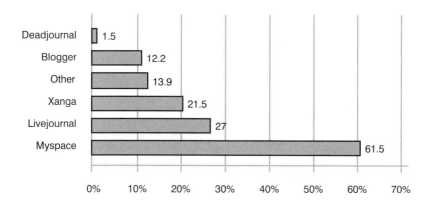

FILE SHARING

Net Generation students are avid consumers of electronic information. Peer-to-peer file sharing allows them to download music, movies, software, games, and documents. Figure 4.10 shows the percentage of students who reported downloading each type of file. About half of the students in the sample (n=3,194) used peer-to-peer file sharing to download music. These data are consistent with reports in the mainstream media that describe how peer-to-peer file sharing has caused a decline in compact disc and online album sales.

Figure 4.10. Net Generation Survey: Percentage of students who reported downloading games, documents, software, movies, videos, and music through peer-to-peer networks (N=6,519).

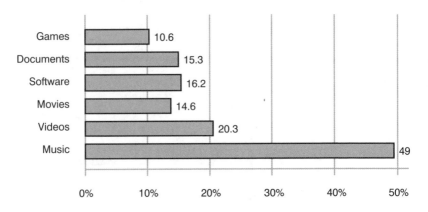

FACEBOOK

Net Generation students have embraced the Facebook phenomenon—hosting profile pages and allowing networking through semiprivate campus networks. We found that 68.5% of students (n=4,461) reported having Facebook accounts. While this percentage was high, now that Facebook is available at all institutions, probably even more Net Gen students are participating. Students who have Facebook accounts (n=4,400) reported typically logging in twice a day (see Figure 4.11).

Figure 4.11. **Net Generation Survey: Number of times students logged on to Facebook each day (n=4,400).**

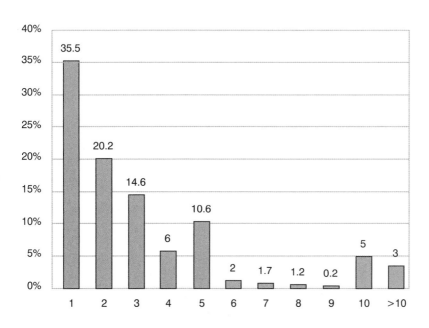

SUMMARY

The Net Generation Survey showed that students are avid users of technology. Net Gen students reported communicating frequently with their parents, often to discuss academics and other school-related topics, including complaints about their classes and issues with advising. They communicate a great deal and spend a lot of time chatting via instant messaging. Interestingly, bloggers spend a great deal of time reading blogs—it's possible that, once connected to the blogosphere, students are hooked. As reported in chapter 3, Net Generation students are prolific multitaskers; this is the case even when they are attempting to do their schoolwork. Adding up all the time students spend using technology, one can see why they spend less time studying than ever before (Jones, 2002). It was also apparent that online pastimes do hurt schoolwork for a subset of the population at rates that were substantially higher than the 14% found by Kubey, Lavin, and Barrows in their 2001 study. It will be important for student affairs professionals to attempt to identify these students in order to create interventions that will enhance their college success.

References

Carnevale, D. (2006, October 6). E-mail is for old people. *Chronicle of Higher Education, 53*(7), A27.

Fallows, D. (2005). *How women and men use the Internet.* Washington, DC: Pew Internet and American Life Project.

Jones, S. (2002). *The Internet goes to college: How students are living in the future with today's technology.* Washington, DC: Pew Internet and American Life Project.

Junco, R. (2005). Technology and today's first-year students. In M. L. Upcraft, J. N. Gardner, B. O. Barefoot, & associates (Eds.), *Meeting challenges and building support: Creating a climate for first-year student success*, (pp. 221–238). San Francisco: Jossey-Bass.

Lenhart, A., & Madden, M. (2005). *Teen content creators and consumers.* Washington, DC: Pew Internet and American Life Project.

Chapter 5

Impact of the Net Generation on the Practice of Student Affairs

W hile trends in student bodies affect all functions of institutions of higher education, divisions of student affairs tend to have the primary responsibility to work directly with students and to educate campus communities about student issues. As part of that role, student affairs professionals have studied Net Generation students—assessing their needs, measuring their learning, and making changes that are needed to better serve these students.

The Net Generation is the most diverse generation in U.S. history. The percentage of citizens from non-White backgrounds has surpassed the 31% reported in the 2000 Census (U.S. Census, 2000). As of 2006, in some areas of the country, minorities are the majority: Latinos are in the majority in New Jersey and are approaching the majority in California and Texas, and African Americans have been in the majority in the District of Columbia since the 1960s (U.S. Census, 2006). At a roundtable discussion for senior student affairs officers in late 2006, the past president of NASPA identified the three most discussed topics in student affairs as mental health issues, parental involvement, and social networking sites such as Facebook (Conneely, 2006). All three issues have evolved as a result of Net Generation students enrolling in college. Understanding student attitudes is a key component of successful student affairs practice.

Enrollments at institutions of higher education are at their highest level of diversity ever (Broido, 2004; DeBard, 2004; Terry, Dukes, Valdez, & Wilson, 2005). The American Council on Education's report *Minorities in Higher Education* (ACE, 2006) noted that the number of minority students on U.S. college and university campuses grew by 50.7% between 1993 and 2003, while the number of White students increased by only 3.4% during the same period. Students of color made up 27.8% of the nearly 17 million students on U.S. college and university campuses in 2003, up from 21.8% in 1993 (ACE, 2006). However, African American and Latino students are still behind their White peers in the rates at which they enroll in college: In the period 2002–04, 47.3% of White high school graduates ages 18–24 years attended college, compared with 41.1% of African Americans and 35.2% of Latinos (ACE, 2006).

Access for students from underrepresented backgrounds is an extremely important topic in higher education; it is becoming harder for students from lower socioeconomic levels to attend four-year colleges, whether public or private. The cost of attending the least expensive public four-year colleges is increasing rapidly, and there is less financial support for higher education from state and federal governments. Fewer students from families with incomes between $30,000 and $50,000 per year received bachelor's degrees in 2004 (11%) than in 1980 (15%). Over the same period, the percentage of students from more affluent families who received degrees rose from 72% to 79% (Burd, 2006).

In describing the Net Generation, this book discusses traditional-aged college students with access to four-year institutions. Literature about working with certain populations of college students who need extra support—such as first-generation college students; racial and ethnic minority students; gay, lesbian, bisexual, and transgender students; students with disabilities; student athletes; and students with at least one immigrant parent—provides detailed information about those populations. Discussions of generational trends often result in generalizations about large groups of people, but the themes that emerge can still provide guidance for higher education leaders (Terry, Dukes, Valdez, & Wilson, 2005).

Evolution of Student Affairs Services

Divisions of student affairs matured at the end of the 20th century and became central functions of institutions of higher education (Sandeen, 2001). Student affairs began to assume responsibility for units such as intercollegiate athletics, campus safety, and academic advising. At the same time, functions such as admissions, financial aid, and registration moved out of the student affairs purview on many campuses and became central functions reporting directly to provosts or vice presidents.

Student affairs operations have become much more specialized in the past 25 years. Several new areas have been created in response to student demand (Sandeen, 2001), such as lesbian, gay, bisexual, and transgender (LGBT) services (Schuh, 2005). As of February 2006, 109 U.S. campuses had professional or graduate assistant staff providing LGBT resources and services, compared with 1 campus in 1971 (National Consortium of Directors of LGBT Resources in Higher Education, 2006). Members of the Net Generation show increasing levels of support for the rights of lesbians and gays, partly because of their familiarity with people who identify as LGBT in their own lives and in the media (Broido, 2004).

Understanding student expectations for their collegiate experiences and providing appropriate services, programs, and facilities is a focus of the practice of student affairs (Bender & Miller, 2005; Miller, Bender, & Schuh, 2005). To develop policies, administrators need to know what students and their parents expect as consumers. Student expectations affect all aspects of the university, not just student affairs. For instance, functions such as the cleanliness and security of facilities change depending on student needs and expectations (Bender & Miller, 2005; Miller, Bender, & Schuh, 2005).

The National Expectations Project conducted by NASPA examined student expectations across various institutional types and published the results in *Promoting Reasonable Expectations* (Miller, Bender, & Schuh, 2005). The study concluded that more attention was needed to help students form accurate and realistic expectations about the college experience, as they often begin college with misperceptions. An example of a misperception is the expectation that the level of academic challenge in college will be similar to high school. Such an expectation may lead a student to blame a poor grade on a faculty member instead of on her or his own lack of preparation (Bender & Miller, 2005; Miller, Bender, & Schuh, 2005).

Safety, Security, and Mental Health Issues

Lowery (2004) identified several ways in which the Net Generation has had an impact on the profession of student affairs, especially in the areas of security and physical and mental health. Net Generation students are more aware of safety and campus crime because they grew up with zero-tolerance policies in the public school systems. Events such as the Columbine shooting on April 20, 1999, and the terrorist attacks of September 11, 2001, increased these students' desire to be sheltered and their tendency to be conventional (Coomes, 2004; DeBard, 2004; Lowery, 2004). Net Generation students expect misconduct to be addressed quickly and decisively (Lowery, 2004). Today, in response to the Jeanne Clery Act, institutions must compile and distribute statistics and information related to campus safety, often through their divisions of student affairs or the campus police. The Net Generation's attention to safety and security is greater than that of previous generations (Howe & Strauss, 2000).

Another shift in student affairs practice involves the increase in services for students with disabilities and those with psychological disorders. Students' willingness to ask for help from adults has contributed to this shift (Lowery, 2004). From 1978 to 1998, the number of first-year college students with disabilities grew from 3% to 9%, and that number continues to increase (National Council on Disability, 2003; see also Wilson, 2004). Many students are diagnosed with learning disabilities during college (National Council on Disability, 2003; Schuh, 2005; Wilson, 2004). Also, more students are coming to campus with psychological and counseling needs (Schuh, 2005).

Counseling center directors report that more students are using their services and are taking psychiatric medications (Lowery, 2004; Schuh, 2005). The American College Health Association (ACHA) surveys college students to evaluate health trends on campuses; in its National College Health Assessment (NCHA) survey, the percentage of students who reported depression and anxiety "in the last school year" increased steadily from 2000 to 2005 (American College Health Association, 2006). Furthermore, 45.7% of the 54,111 students in the spring 2005 survey reported being so depressed that it was difficult to function (American College Health Association, 2006). Students also reported that their mental health issues impacted their academics with 16.3% reporting that depression or anxiety affected their academic performance. Accommodations for these students are often coordinated through student affairs, and those from the Net Generation are willing to use those services (Lowery, 2004).

TECHNOLOGY

Net Generation students are comfortable with constant multitasking; they can "juggle e-mail on their Blackberrys while talking on cellphones while trolling online" (Armour, 2005, p. C1). Students from the Net Generation spend less time on one task at a time, preferring to manage multiple tasks at once (Carlson, 2005). On the Net Generation Survey, 91.9% of IM users reported that they IM while performing other computer tasks (see chapter 4). Moreover, data from the Pew Internet and American Life Project show that Net Generation students multitask at one and a half times the rate of Gen Xers and twice the rate of Boomers (Shiu & Lenhart, 2004). Student affairs has had to shift its practice to reach these multitasking students.

If Net Generation students encounter any delays in response to their inquiries, they perceive that institutions are not meeting their needs (Lowery, 2004). Those who work on college campuses are increasingly expected to respond quickly to e-mail, in addition to traditional face-to-face and telephone contacts; these expectations have added to the administrative burden and have not necessarily been accompanied by an increase in resources. In addition, college officials across the country are reporting that more students are missing important e-mail messages about deadlines, class cancellations, and events, because the students no longer prefer e-mail (Carnevale, 2006). Net Generation students have developed a preference for using synchronous methods of communication like instant messaging (see chapter 4).

One example of the increase in demand without an increase in resources is the University of Florida's (UF's) Academic Advising Center (2005), which had significant increases in telephone, e-mail, and group contacts (advising sessions with multiple students) from 2001 through

2004 (see Table 5.1), while the rate of individual face-to-face advising stayed the same. There was no increase in the number of advisors to handle the additional workload.

Table 5.1. Increase in phone, e-mail, and group contacts for the University of Florida Academic Advising Center.

Year	Contacts by Phone/E-mail/ Groups
2001	27,937
2002	29,752
2003	38,227
2004	39,563

Source: University of Florida Academic Advising Center

The number of e-mails sent after traditional working hours—when most students are still awake and online—has increased, and members of the Net Generation expect a fast response (Oblinger, 2003). In a discussion with student leaders at a large private university in the Northeast, the authors discovered that these students expected student affairs administrators to "definitely" respond to their overnight e-mail messages by noon the next day at the very latest. When they were told that university administrators juggle a variety of tasks and might not be able to answer e-mail messages so quickly, the students conceded that a response by 4 p.m. the next day would be acceptable.

Web-based services are becoming more important for effective delivery of support services for students, but student affairs is still catching up with the best practices. For example, it is often necessary for students to log on to several systems with multiple user names and passwords; the Web sites of different departments on the same campus may look very different and navigate differently; and some transactions may require an in-person visit to complete (Kleeman, 2005). Kleeman (2005) said that

91

student affairs professionals need to realize that the Web is a virtual place where they can develop community and manage relationships across organizational units. He suggested that student affairs divisions should lead their campuses in restructuring Web sites to better meet the needs of students.

Campuses are constantly exploring new ways to work with technology as students continue to use technology in more and different ways. For example, communication with students has moved from print newsletters to e-mail and Web sites. Some institutions are exploring other ways to communicate with students, such as text messaging. One program, Mobile Campus 101, allows students to select the organizations, clubs, faculty, restaurants, and stores from which they want to receive text messages (Mobile Campus Web site, 2006). Lowery (2004) stated that the use of technology "holds the greatest promise for responding to [the Net Generation's] preference for efficient services" (p. 95).

FACEBOOK AND OTHER SOCIAL NETWORKING WEB SITES

Social networking Web sites and how college students use them is a frequent topic of discussion among student affairs professionals. Several Web sites—such as MySpace, Friendster, and Facebook—allow users to create profile pages that include their interests, hobbies, and additional personal details, as well as photos of themselves and others. As a result, online privacy issues are becoming a hot topic for student affairs professionals and the Net Generation (Dahne, 2006).

Facebook is a very popular social networking Web site. It is the seventh-most visited Web site in the United States—as of September 2006, more than 9.5 million people were registered through 2,200 college networks (Facebook, 2006). Facebook users "can link to others' profiles by designating them as friends, form and join groups of like-minded users, announce parties, post photo albums, and write notes on other users' walls (message boards that appear alongside their profiles)" (Read, 2006).

In the Net Generation Survey, 68.5% of students reported having Facebook accounts, and the typical user logs on twice a day (see chapter 4). Two thirds of registered Facebook users spend an average of 20 minutes on the site daily (Facebook, 2006). Student affairs professionals have attempted to regulate or advise students on the use of Facebook and similar Web sites, especially the practice of posting detailed personal information online. Serious issues related to stalking, sexual assault, and defamation have affected how university officials interact with students about Facebook (Conneely, 2006; Read, 2006). Some schools have issued guidelines urging common sense and awareness of privacy issues, and warning students that posting photographs and personal information can lead to problems (Dahne, 2006; Read, 2006).

Several issues involving social networking sites such as Facebook are currently affecting student affairs divisions, making this a hot topic at meetings of student affairs professionals (Conneely, 2006). The issues of legal liability for monitoring the sites or proceeding with judicial action based on students' postings are being considered across the nation (Conneely, 2006; Dahne, 2006). Questions include whether university officials should be monitoring activities and photographs on Facebook; how to react to evidence of illegal or inappropriate content placed by students or staff; and how much education on appropriate use of such Web sites is necessary (Conneely, 2006; Dahne, 2006). If institutions aggressively search for violations of conduct codes on such Web sites, they may create expectations that they should be doing so as part of the regular course of business and may find themselves with additional legal responsibility.

Other issues related to Facebook have affected student affairs practice as well. Students who are moving into residence halls are often able to check out their potential roommates on Facebook, and record numbers of them are asking to change roommates before they even get to school (Farrell, 2006). Students are harassing and defaming others, or otherwise using the social networking Web sites to give inappropriate or problematic information to the entire public (Conneely, 2006; Dahne, 2006). On the other hand, Facebook offers many benefits for student affairs divisions; for example, enabling the creation of study groups and advertising department-sponsored programs (Conneely, 2006; Mastrodicasa, 2006).

PARENTS OF THE NET GENERATION

The role of parents has drastically shifted with the newest generation of college students. As described in the Howe and Strauss (2000) definition of the Net Generation, these students are both special and sheltered, and their parents are part of the mix (Lowery, 2004; Wilson, 2004). Because of their unique parenting style, these parents have been referred to as "helicopter parents" by student affairs researchers and practitioners (Terry, Dukes, Valdez, & Wilson, 2005). They "hover" over their children and are involved in issues that previous generations would have considered as belonging solely to the students. Particularly aggressive helicopter parents—"Black Hawks"—are so involved with their children's educations that they have been known to write papers for them and create their schedules.

94

Compared with parents of previous generations, Net Generation parents interact with their children much more frequently, and for different reasons (Keppler, Mullendore, & Carey, 2005). Typically, student affairs officers are responsible for working with parents. In a study at a large public university in the Southeast, approximately half of the student respondents (the vast majority of whom were from the Net Generation) said they spoke with a parent once a day. More than a quarter of the respondents said they listed their parents' address with the university rather than their local address, so that their parents could handle university mail directly (Mastrodicasa & Kepic, 2005). In addition, 36.2% of the respondents had changed their course selections after discussions with parents (Mastrodicasa & Kepic, 2005).

Data from the Net Generation Survey echoed the Mastrodicasa & Kepic (2005) results. Net Generation students reported speaking with their parents more than one-and-a-half times a day on average (see chapter 4). These students reported that they frequently discussed issues that related to the purpose of student affairs with their parents—75.7% discussed issues related to academic success, 66.5% discussed their social life, and 30.1% discussed complaints about their living arrangements. Given that 94.1% of Net Generation students have cell phones and that they speak with their parents frequently, it is no surprise that student affairs professionals often learn about a student problem directly from a parent before they hear about it from their staff or from the student.

An issue that frequently involves parents is the Federal Educational Rights and Privacy Act (FERPA), which protects students' educational records. Net Generation parents frequently contact their children's colleges and universities seeking information from the records (Lowery, 2005; 2006). Under FERPA, written consent is required to release student records to a third party, including a parent. However, colleges and universities may develop policies that allow them to share information with parents without written consent in the following cases: (a) release of records to the parents of a dependent student; (b) release of records in health and safety emergencies; (c) parental notification for alcohol violations; and (d) release to the public of information regarding crimes of violence. As a recommended best practice, each institution and its student affairs division should determine its campus philosophy and policy for working with parents under FERPA (Lowery, 2005; 2006).

In light of the potential difficulties posed by helicopter parents, it is recommended that institutions seek to partner with them rather than at-

95

tempt to fend them off: "Providing opportunities for parents to participate in the college experience can pay huge dividends in terms of increased student success, institutional financial support, and enhanced public relations" (Keppler et al., 2005, p. xi). Numerous opportunities exist to capture parents' energy and interest by creating parent-specific resources and information to be given to them at orientation, through direct mail, or on Web sites, as well as parent handbooks and programmatic opportunities such as family weekends and parent councils (Keppler et al., 2005; Lehman, 2005). Some campuses contact parents to encourage their support of students during the first year or send them gifts, such as the UF Seasons of Adjustment calendar (UF Division of Student Affairs, 2005).

The opposite tactic is to treat parents as a nuisance and encourage their exclusion from some aspects of students' decision-making processes. Some institutions hire student "bouncers" to "intercept" parents who are determined to make decisions for their children during orientation activities. For instance, the University of Vermont (UVM) places highly trained student bouncers at strategic locations to prevent parents from entering advising sessions and student discussions about sex and alcohol (Willis, 2005). The University of California at Santa Barbara (UCSB) has a similar program, in which orientation staff keep parents away from students while they register; the staff explain what the students are doing and provide details about academic advising (Willis, 2005). It is too soon to know which of these tactics (encouraging parents' participation or excluding them) works best, as these programs—and the Net Generation students and parents—are relatively new phenomena on campus.

Summary

The issues facing student affairs have evolved as different generations of college students have arrived on campus. Current issues reflect the arrival of the Net Generation. Topics such as mental health, parental involvement, and social networking Web sites have provided new challenges to the resources and responses of student affairs divisions, and more issues are sure to emerge. Understanding students' expectations concerning the college experience and effectively supporting them in their persistence to graduation is crucial for student affairs professionals working with any generation of students. To fulfill this role, professionals must stay informed about the trends that affect today's college students, through the literature and through contacts with colleagues at their own and other institutions. The issues that face student affairs professionals are continually evolving as the students themselves change, and this process is accelerated by rapid advancements in technology.

RECOMMENDATIONS

In general, Net Generation students came of age in family environments in which they were sheltered and supported, with parents who have always been actively engaged in their welfare. These students are accustomed to being protected by their parents or guardians. As they enter college, they expect (perhaps even on a subconscious level) to be protected in a similar manner. At the same time, their parents assume that the university in general and student affairs professionals in particular will act *in loco parentis* to take care of their children. Net Generation students and their parents expect student affairs professionals to assume this role; however, the professionals are used to working with more independent students who have a different worldview. The following recommendations will help student affairs professionals work in ways that will be most beneficial to Net Gen students:

97

   Campus safety officers and administrators should understand Net Generation students' need to feel safe. Because of their desire to be protected (see chapter 1) and because of the historical events of their time, Net Gen students are willing to conform if it means having a more orderly and safe environment. Campus policies and procedures should reflect this mind-set.

☐ The increase in the numbers of students with disabilities (9% of incoming first-year students reported having a disability in 2003 (National Council on Disability, 2003)) and mental health issues (the percentage of college students who reported anxiety or depression in the previous year increased steadily from 2000 to 2005 (American College Health Association, 2006)) should be met with an increase in the number of disability services and counseling professionals on campus. Counseling and disability services should engage in regular and direct communication for seamless provision of accommodations and services for students with physical disabilities and psychological disorders.

☐ Student affairs departments should engage in programmatic efforts to educate students about the implications of posting sensitive, personal, and potentially harmful information on Internet profile pages such as MySpace or Facebook. While many Net Gen students say they are aware of the consequences of posting inappropriate or sensitive personal information online, it is clear that some still engage in risky online behavior.

☐ Plans for technology expenditures on campus should include student input. Student technology use trends should be assessed frequently, as new technologies are quickly outdated. Support for improving the technology skills of academic and student affairs professionals should be readily available.

☞ Student affairs departments should recognize the Net Generation's desire for quick responses to e-mail and voice mail. Published guidelines for communication times will help Net Gen students understand the multifaceted demands on student affairs professionals. Hosted online chats after normal business hours allow students to ask questions in a forum that is familiar to them. University-sanctioned and -maintained blogs for various student affairs areas allow students to get answers to frequently asked questions, stay current with university news, and ask specific questions of student affairs officers. Some universities, such as the University of Florida, have created a wiki (a Web site that allows users to add and edit content) to engage students in a familiar modality and to provide students with university information (Moritz & Jacobson, 2007).

☞ Student affairs should include Net Gen parents in the orientation process in a way that helps them feel that their needs are being addressed. Other methods of partnering with parents should be used, such as parent handbooks, Web sites, and family weekends. Partnering with parents allows student affairs professionals to enlist parental support and can prove to be extremely helpful. In this sense, parents can become an extension of student affairs by providing information, feedback, and guidance to students.

99

REFERENCES

American College Health Association. (2006). National College Health Assessment Web Summary. Retrieved October 4, 2006, from http://www.acha.org/projects_programs/ncha_sampledata.cfm

American Council on Education. (2006). *Minorities in higher education: Twenty-second annual report.* Washington, DC: Author.

Armour, S. (2005, November 7). Generation Y: They've arrived at work with a new attitude. *USA Today*, p. C1.

Bender, B. E., & Miller, T. E. (Spring, 2005). Student expectations and institutional realities: Creating connections to enhance student success. *Leadership Exchange, 3*(1), 18–21.

Burd, S. (2006, June 9). Working class students feel the pinch. *Chronicle of Higher Education, 52*(40), A20.

Broido, E. M. (2004). Understanding diversity in millennial students. In M. D. Coomes & R. DeBard (Eds.), *Serving the millennial generation: New directions for student services, no. 106* (pp. 73–85). San Francisco: Jossey-Bass.

Carlson, S. (2005, October 7). The net generation goes to college. *Chronicle of Higher Education 52*(7), A34.

Carnevale, D. (2006, October 6). E-mail is for old people. *Chronicle of Higher Education, 53*(7), A27.

Conneely, J. (2006, November 5). Senior Student Affairs Officers Round-table—Facebook and MySpace: What are current trends and implications? Session presented at national meeting of Southern Association for College Student Affairs (SACSA).

Coomes, M. D. (2004). Understanding the historical and cultural influences that shape generations. In M. D. Coomes & R. DeBard (Eds.), *Serving* the millennial generation: New directions for student services, no. 106 (pp. 17–31). San Francisco: Jossey-Bass.

Dahne, M. (2006, Spring). What's the fuss over Facebook? *Leadership Exchange*, *4*(1), 24-25.

DeBard, R. (2004). Millennials coming to college. In M. D. Coomes & R. DeBard (Eds.), *Serving the millennial generation: New directions for student services, no. 106* (pp. 33–45). San Francisco: Jossey-Bass.

Facebook. (2006). Press: Facebook overview. Retrieved September 27, 2006, from http://www.facebook.com/press.php

Farrell, E. F. (2006, September 1). Judging roommates by their Facebook cover. *Chronicle of Higher Education, 53*(2), A53.

Howe, N., & Strauss, W. (2000). *Millennials rising: The next great generation.* New York: Vintage Books.

Junco, R. (2005). Technology and today's first-year students. In M. L. Upcraft, J. N. Gardner, B. O. Barefoot, & associates (Eds.), *Meeting challenges and building support: Creating a climate for first-year student success*, (pp. 221–238). San Francisco: Jossey-Bass.

Keppler, K., Mullendore, R. H., & Carey, A. (2005). *Partnering with the parents of today's college students*. Washington, DC: NASPA.

Kleeman, G. L. (2005, Winter). A cross-functional team approach to supporting Web-based student services. *Leadership Exchange*, *3*(4), 18–21.

Lehman, G. (2005, November 20). Parents are encouraged to interact, not overreact. *Miami Herald*, p. 3EG.

Lowery, J. W. (2004). Student affairs for a new generation. In M. D. Coomes & R. DeBard (Eds.), *Serving the millennial generation: New directions for student services, no. 106* (pp. 87–99). San Francisco: Jossey-Bass.

Lowery, J. W. (2005). Legal issues regarding partnering with parents: Misunderstood federal laws and potential sources of institutional liability. In K.

Keppler., R. H. Mullendore, & A. Carey (Eds.), *Partnering with the parents of today's college students* (pp. 43–51). Washington, DC: NASPA.

Lowery, J. W. (2006, Spring). FERPA and communicating with parents. *Leadership Exchange*, 4(1), 22.

Mastrodicasa, J. M. (2006, Spring). Facebooking: The new fad in campus communication. *CLAS Notes*, p. 3. (University of Florida College of Liberal Arts and Sciences).

Mastrodicasa, J. M., & Kepic, G. (2005, October). *Parents gone wild*. Paper presented at meeting of National Academic Advising Association, Las Vegas, NV.

Miller, T. E., Bender, B. E., & Schuh, J. H. (2005). *Promoting reasonable expectations: Aligning student and institutional views of the college experience*. San Francisco: Jossey-Bass.

Mobile Campus. (2006). Mobile Campus 101. Retrieved June 9, 2006, from http://mobilecampus.com

Moritz, M., & Jacobson, Z. (2007). *Gatorpedia.* Retrieved January 30, 2007, from http://www.gatorpedia.com/index.php/Main_Page

National Consortium of Directors of LGBT Resources in Higher Education (2006, Spring). *Consortium Newsletter, 2,* 1.

National Council on Disability. (2003, September 15). *People with disabilities and postsecondary education*. Retrieved August 11, 2006, from http://www.ncd.gov/newsroom/publications/2003/education.htm

Oblinger, D. (2003) Boomers, Gen-Xers, & Millennials: Understanding the "new students." *EDUCAUSE Review, 38*(4), 37–47.

Read, B. (2006, January 20). Think before you share. *Chronicle of Higher Education*, A38.

Sandeen, A. (2001). Organizing student affairs divisions. In R. B. Winston, Jr., D.G. Creamer, T. K. Miller, & Associates (Eds.), *The professional student affairs administrator: Educator, leader, and manager*, (pp. 181–209). New York: Brunner-Routledge.

Shiu, E., & Lenhart, A. (2004). *How Americans use instant messaging.* Washington, DC: Pew Internet and American Life Project.

Schuh, J. H. (2005). Student support services. In M. L. Upcraft, J. N. Gardner, B. O. Barefoot, & associates (Eds.), *Meeting challenges and building support: Creating a climate for first-year student success*, (pp. 428–444). San Francisco: Jossey-Bass.

Terry, R. B., Dukes, C. M., Valdez, L. E., & Wilson, A. (2005). Changing demographics and diversity in higher education. In K. Keppler., R. H. Mullendore, & A. Carey (Eds.), *Partnering with the parents of today's college students* (pp. 11–19). Washington, DC: NASPA.

United States Census. (2006). Estimates of the population by race alone or in combination and Hispanic or Latino origin for the United States and states: July 1, 2005. Retrieved November 12, 2006, from http://www. census.gov/Press-Release/www/2006/cb06-123table1.xls

United States Census. (2000). Total population by age, race, and Hispanic or Latino origin for the United States: 2000. Retrieved November 12, 2006, from http://www.census.gov/population/cen2000/phc-t9/tab01.pdf

University of Florida Academic Advising Center. (2005). *Student contact statistics.* Gainesville, FL: Author.

University of Florida Division of Student Affairs. (2005). Seasons of adjustment: Parent's guide to the first-year experience. Retrieved December 8, 2005, from http://www.ufsa.ufl.edu/ovp/pdf/05-06UFCalfinal.pdf

Willis, E. (2005, July 22). Parent trap. *Chronicle of Higher Education*, A4.

Wilson, M. E. (2004). Teaching, learning, and millennial students. In M. D. Coomes & R. DeBard (Eds.), *Serving the millennial generation: New directions for student services, no. 106* (pp. 59–71). San Francisco: Jossey-Bass.

Chapter 6

Net Generation Career and Workplace Issues

Already the fastest-growing segment of the workforce, the Net Generation will eventually expand to nearly 70 million workers (Armour, 2005). Entry-level hiring is expected to grow by more than 17% in 2007—the fourth consecutive year of double-digit increases in hiring (Gerdes, 2006). This influx of new employees—who approach work with a different perspective than the Silent Generation, Boomers, and Generation Xers—is already starting to cause friction in the workplace: 60% of employers report intergenerational tensions among employees (Armour, 2005; see also Gerdes, 2006).

In a number of significant ways, employees from the Net Generation espouse different values than their other-generation colleagues. At the same time, older employers may not respect the abilities of their younger co-workers (Armour, 2005; Gerdes, 2006, Raines, 2002). New organizational models are needed to accommodate the work styles of the Net Generation (Lowery, 2005). Student affairs professionals, especially those who focus on career development, face many challenges in preparing this generation for the world of work. This chapter focuses on how the unique qualities of the Net Generation influence these students' career paths and how career services professionals can guide them in their career development.

VALUES AND CHARACTERISTICS OF THE GENERATIONS

Generational studies show that the experiences and events of a generation affect members' attitudes, values, and habits as adults. A peer personality is created as members share developmental stages, beliefs, behaviors, and perceived membership in a common group (Coomes & DeBard, 2004). In this chapter, we discuss four groups of employees: the Silent Generation, Boomers, Generation Xers, and the Net Generation. Members of the Silent Generation were born between 1925 and 1942; Boomers were born between 1943 and 1960; Generation Xers were born between 1961 and 1981; and members of the Net Generation were born in 1982 or later. As was discussed in Chapter 1, these dates are rough guidelines as generations are defined more by shared experiences and a common location in history.

Members of the Silent Generation (born between 1925 and 1942) came of age around the time of World War II and may have been old enough to remember struggling through the Great Depression. They have worked hard and believe in paying their dues and maintaining job security (Center for Generational Studies, 2005). Silent Generation employees are valued by their superiors because, unlike employees from other genera-tions, they tend not to question authority. Many of these people's parents lost their jobs during the Great Depression; therefore, they are grateful to be employed. Members of the Silent Generation consider employment a privilege, not a right, and they act accordingly—they are deeply loyal to their employers and feel a sense of duty to work hard for their companies, just as they worked hard for their country when they were in the military (Zemke, Raines, & Filipczak, 2000; Center for Generational Studies, 2005; Raines, 2002; Reesor & Schlabach, 2006).

The Boomers (born between 1943 and 1960) came of age during an expansion of the economy that resulted in a great deal of focus and marketing attention on their generation. Boomers tended to have a similar sense of duty and personal identity with their jobs as the Silent Generation, and they spent less time at home with their families than later generations (Center for Generational Studies, 2005). Boomers are very optimistic, focused on teamwork, and have worked hard to accumulate wealth, even at a cost to their personal lives. Older Boomers are much more achievement-oriented than their late-Boomer counterparts. The term "yuppie" (for young urban professional) was coined to describe the fashionable and trendy early Boomers who were focused on success. The later Boomers are more skeptical about the idea that hard work is rewarded, possibly because they entered the workforce during a time of mass downsizing in the Reagan era; these Boomers sometimes identify more with Gen Xers than with their early Boomer counterparts (Zemke, Raines, & Filipczak, 2000; see also Raines, 2002; Reesor & Schlabach, 2006).

107

Generation Xers (born between 1961 and 1981) tend to be much more independent than other generations, as many were raised in dual-career families and were latchkey kids (Reesor & Schlabach, 2006). They focus on creating balance between family and work, and prefer to control their own careers rather than allowing employers to shape them (Center for Generational Studies, 2005). Because of their desire for balance, they like flexible hours and informality in the workplace; they often prefer to work alone (Reesor & Schlabach, 2006). Members of Generation X are often negatively stereotyped as "slackers." The earlier Generation X members joined the workforce after the upheaval of the downsizing era, at a time when employers did not offer much stability for employees, especially recent hires. In addition, Gen Xers have a need to belong to family systems and are skeptical of authority because of their experience with the unethical behavior of national Boomer leaders. The disillusionment with their leaders, combined with the historical backdrop of their generation, is the foundation of what is labeled the "slacker" mentality. Later Gen Xers continue to be sought after in the workforce because of their familiarity with technology. Although they are not generally as technically proficient as the Net Generation, Xers grew up with computers, microwaves, VCRs, and so on, and learned to use them (Zemke, Raines, & Filipczak, 2000; see also Raines, 2002; Reesor & Schlabach, 2006).

Members of the Net Generation (born in and after 1982) have characteristics that blend some of the best qualities of the previous generations. Because they grew up belonging to teams and working in groups, Net Gen students, like their Boomer parents, believe in teamwork. Because they have pressured themselves to succeed and believe that their short-term accomplishments will lead to long-term success, members of the Net Generation are hard-working and self-confident like the Silent Generation. Net Gen employees trust authority and may be the next group of employees to be "loved" by their superiors (Zemke, Raines, & Filipczak, 2000). Net Generation employees are also quite adept at using technology and are avid multitaskers, making them especially suited to fill jobs in the technology sector, which continues to grow beyond the supply of available employees (Zemke, Raines, & Filipczak; see also Raines, 2002; Reesor & Schlabach, 2006).

APPROACHES TOWARD WORK

The four groups have unique approaches toward work. Members of the Silent Generation are disciplined, hard workers who appreciate order

108

and a job well done. Boomers are driven, service-oriented team players who do not want to be micromanaged and who "live to work." Generation X workers are independent, self-reliant, unimpressed by authority, and focused on self-development; they "work to live." Members of the Net Generation are self-confident, optimistic, competent, outspoken, collaborative in the work setting, and respond well to authority (Alberta Learning Information Service, 2005). Howe and Strauss (2000) described the Net Generation as team-oriented, so employers who encourage teamwork and collaboration will attract Net Generation workers (Alsop, 2006).

Members of each generation have opinions about how other generations function in the workplace. Table 6.1 lists some of these views.

Table 6.1. **Conflicting views in the multigenerational workplace.**

Silent Generation

- ☞ Boomers accuse them of being inflexible and overly cautious.

- ☞ Gen Xers are frustrated at their lack of technology savvy— some do not even communicate via e-mail.

- ☞ Net Generation workers think they are slow.

Boomers

- ☞ The Silent Generation consider Boomers to be self-absorbed.

- ☞ Gen Xers perceive them as micromanagers.

- ☞ Net Generation workers think they are uptight.

Generation X

- ☞ The Silent Generation think Gen Xers are rude.

- ☞ Boomers consider them slackers.

- ☞ Net Generation workers complain that Gen Xers are cynical, aloof, and pessimistic.

Net Generation

- ☞ The Silent Generation tend to patronize Net Generation workers because they are often the same age as their grandchildren.

- ☞ Boomers think they require too much attention.

- ☞ Gen Xers complain that they are indulged, self-absorbed, Pollyanna-ish, and naïve.

Source: Reesor & Schlabach, 2006, p. 18.

To explain differences among generations in the workplace, DeBard (2004) assembled a list of traits, tendencies, and generational values in 12 areas for Boomers, Generation Xers, and the Net Generation (Table 6.2). In compiling his list, DeBard (2004) cited the work of Howe and Strauss (2000); Lancaster and Stillman (2002); and Zemke, Raines, and Filipczak (2000).

Table 6.2. Comparing generational traits, tendencies, and values.

Views Toward	Boomers	Gen Xers	Net Generation
Level of trust	Confident of self, not authority	Low toward authority	High toward authority
Loyalty to institutions	Cynical	Considered naïve	Committed
Most admire	Taking charge	Creating enterprise	Following a hero of integrity
Career Goals	Build a stellar career	Build a portable career	Build parallel careers
Rewards	Title and the corner office	Freedom not to do	Meaningful work
Parent-child involvement	Receding	Distant	Intruding
Having children	Controlled	Doubtful	Definite
Family life	Indulged as children	Alienated as children	Protected as children
Education	Freedom of expression	Pragmatic	Structure of accountability
Evaluation	Once a year with documentation	"Sorry, but how am I doing?"	Feedback whenever I want it
Political orientation	Attack oppression	Apathetic, individual	Crave community
The big question	What does it mean?	Does it work?	How do we build it?

Source: DeBard, 2004, p. 40.

111

Different values emerge when people are engaged in a multigenerational work setting. Members of the Silent Generation value respect, loyalty, and experience; Boomers value recognition; Generation Xers value flexibility, honesty, feedback, and work-life balance; and members of the Net Generation value strong leadership, concern for community, structure, fair play, and diversity (Alberta Learning Information Service, 2005; Mastrodicasa & Junco, 2006). These values often produce tension and conflict between generations at work (Armour, 2005; Gerdes, 2006; Lowery, 2004; NAS Recruitment Communications, 2006; Raines, 2002; Reesor & Schlabach, 2006).

Each generation has different attitudes toward hours of work and systems of recognition and rewards, which create conflicts, challenges, and opportunities for the generations to learn from each other (Armour, 2005; NAS Recruitment Communications, 2006; Raines, 2002; Reesor & Schlabach, 2006). Members of the Net Generation—with their consumer mentality—have high expectations for themselves and their employers, similar to the expectations they have for their colleges. They seek managers who are direct, just, and highly engaged in their professional development (Alberta Learning Information Service, 2005; Armour, 2005; Howe & Strauss, 2000). As employees, they expect constant feedback from their employers (Alsop, 2006; Gerdes, 2006; NAS Recruitment Communications, 2006). They prefer to quit a job rather than advocate changes in the workplace (Jayson, 2006; Sacks, 2006).

Members of the Net Generation are entering the workforce at a time of rapid technological advancements, and these advancements have directly affected the way this generation works. One example is telecommuting. The number of telecommuters doubled between 2000 and 2005; today, almost 25% of U.S. workers telecommute at least once a month (Margulius, 2006). Worldwide, 80 million employees telecommuted at least one day a month in 2005, up from 38 million in 2000 (Margulius, 2006). Telecommuting will undoubtedly continue to grow in popularity as more tech-savvy Net Generation employees enter the workforce.

The Center for Generational Studies (2005) has suggested that media influence, societal expectations, and the natural impatience of youth may explain the job expectations of members of the Net Generation; and these expectations have not necessarily been met in the workplace. They want detailed descriptions of their duties up front, and they want a timetable for promotions (Alsop, 2006). Although corporate leaders are revered in our society, young employees are disillusioned by the mundane and repetitive nature of many work assignments (Center for Generational Studies, 2005), which they consider irrelevant, frustrating, and a waste of their time (Alsop,

2006; Sacks, 2006). They believe that such tasks should be handled using technology (Center for Generational Studies, 2005).

Because members of the Net Generation have lived structured lives, with play dates and other organized activities, they prefer to have clearly defined policies and responsibilities with few ambiguities (Alsop, 2006; Gerdes, 2006; Raines, 2002; Reesor & Schlabach, 2006). When they enter the workforce, they may be startled to find that they do not get the instant rewards they have come to expect as a result of being the focus of so much attention and encouragement from their parents (Keppler, Mullendore, & Carey, 2005; Lehman, 2005). As one Net Generation member said, "We're surprised we have to work for our money. We want the corner office right away. It seems like our parents just groomed us. Anything is possible. We had karate class, soccer practice, everything. But they deprived us of social skills" (Armour, 2005, p. C1).

Members of the Net Generation expect to be employed in a number of different jobs with a number of different employers, so they are often not focused on finding a first job in their desired career path (Armour, 2005; Jayson, 2006; Sacks, 2006). They want jobs that are relevant, make an impact, and offer a variety of experiences (Alsop, 2006). Members of the Net Generation value social responsibility and seek companies with those values (Alsop, 2006; DeBard, 2004; NAS Recruitment Communications, 2006).

113

The values of potential employees are an issue for recruiters, and professional associations such as the National Association of Colleges and Employers are conducting research on the Net Generation at work. As the largest generation in history arrives in the workplace, its attitudes are affecting how businesses recruit and retain employees. For example, on the basis of focus group input, Lockheed Martin Corporation stepped up recruiting, increased vacation time, and improved its mentoring program during the past three years—and applications for entry-level positions nearly tripled as a result (Gerdes, 2006).

Business recruiters report that Net Generation candidates may delay decisions about taking a job so they can use offers as leverage with other companies. A relatively new phenomenon reported in conversations with recruiters is that Net Generation candidates accept positions, then back out of those commitments to accept better offers from other employers; recruiters have reported that this happens as late as the week before the start date. Researchers and consultants agree that this practice signals a shift in generational attitudes: Net Generation candidates do not have the same feeling as members of other generations about accepting employment offers and making commitments. Net Gen attitudes are especially different from the expectations of the Boomer and Gen X recruiters who are hiring these candidates. This behavior on the part of Net Generation recruits has caused resentment among employers regarding what they perceive to be insensitivity, lack of loyalty, and a sense of entitlement (Armour, 2005; Eubanks, 2006; Gerdes, 2006; Lancaster & Stillman, 2002; Sacks, 2006).

Researchers have begun to explore Net Generation employees' career values to determine how they differ from those of employees of other generations. A survey of more than 27,000 undergraduate students by Universum Communications, a recruitment and retention consulting firm, found that Net Generation career goals were to balance personal and professional lives (59%), pursue further education (46%), build sound financial bases (32%), and contribute to society (27%; Green, 2006). The survey found that while Gen Xers considered financial strength to be the most important criterion in selecting an employer, members of the Net Generation valued high ethical standards most. And although base salaries are important to Net Generation employees, strong health care plans outranked salaries as a top priority (Green, 2006). The ability to balance personal and professional lives is a crucial component of recruiting and retaining Net Generation employees (Green, 2006; Sacks, 2006), but fellow employees from other generations often resent the accommodations made to retain their successors (Sacks, 2006).

The events of September 11, 2001, had a tremendous impact on the Net Generation's sense of civil order and patriotism. In 2001, very few of the top 100 employers were government agencies; now, however, government agencies (the Department of State, the Federal Bureau of Investigation, and the Central Intelligence Agency) are among the top five desired employers. Television shows about government work have been popular with Net Generation students—24, *West Wing*, *Without a Trace*, and similar programs highlight service to the government. The positive media portrayal of government service has coincided with increased participation in community service by the Net Generation to create a revived interest in public service (Green, 2006; Universum Communications, 2006).

Having fun and being stimulated at work are important to the Net Generation (Center for Generational Studies, 2005; Green, 2006; Reesor & Schlabach, 2006). The top two ideal employers identified by members of the Net Generation in the Universum Communications survey were the Walt Disney Company and Google; their popularity is based on the perception that they provide fun work atmospheres and encourage play (Green, 2006; Universum Communications, 2006). And finally, one small aspect of attracting Net Generation employees is implementation of casual dress codes (Armour, 2005).

Satisfying Net Generation employees means focusing on them as individuals, an approach that aligns with Howe and Strauss's (2000) description of this generation as special, sheltered, team-oriented, achieving, and confident. NAS Recruitment Communications (2006) states that successful retention of these employees depends on several factors: (a) good relationships with bosses and co-workers; (b) good incomes; (c) opportunities for growth; (d) opportunities to show off skills and receive recognition for good performance; (e) challenging daily work; (f) flexible schedules for social and personal time; and (g) casual dress environments.

TECHNOLOGY IN THE NET GENERATION WORKPLACE

The Net Generation's level of comfort with technology is much higher than that of any previous generation (Armour, 2005; Reesor & Schlabach, 2006). Marc Prensky, a consultant, states that "their preference is for sharing, staying connected, instantaneity, multi-tasking, assembling random information into patterns, and using technology in new ways. Their challenge to the established way of doing things in the business world has already started" (as cited in Rainie, 2006). While these preferences offer great opportunities for moving forward in a modern way, they can create challenges for those who are less comfortable with technology. For example, members of the Net Generation expect to solve problems—such as determining what content should be on a Web site—in a virtual world, while members of other generations may prefer phone calls or in-person meetings (Armour, 2005).

Net Generation employees, like Net Generation students, are quite adept at constant multitasking (Junco, 2005). Net Generation employees multitask substantially more than their Gen X and Boomer co-workers (Shiu & Lenhart, 2004). In the Net Generation Survey, 75% of Net Gen students said they used IM and did schoolwork at the same time (see chapter 4). These students and employees say they perform better when they are multitasking, but supervisors from other generations tend to prefer employees to focus on one task at a time (Junco, 2005; Rainie, 2006).

Because of the influx of Net Generation employees, employers have increasingly monitored and restricted personal use of technology and some employers use special hardware and software to block access to certain Web sites. The ePolicy Institute and the American Management Association (2004) found that 60% of the 840 businesses they surveyed monitored employee e-mail and more than 10% monitored employee IMs. The increase in technology use in the workplace has led many businesses to create and enforce e-mail and Internet use policies. Recently, employers have suspended and even fired employees for personal use of company e-mail and the Internet (Zetter & Albro, 2006).

Another sign that Net Generation employees are driving changes in policy is the change in how employers are training their new workforce. Workplace training has shifted to reflect the learning style of the Net Generation. For example, Marriott International is changing its information dissemination to short sound bites in the form of training podcasts so workers can download information to their laptops, cell phones, and iPods (Sacks, 2006).

PARENTS OF NET GENERATION EMPLOYEES

Parents play crucial roles in the lives of their Net Generation children, and those relationships have become part of the workplace. Sometimes the helicopter parent attitudes seen in the postsecondary setting continue into the workplace. Sacks (2006) gave one example of a 22-year-old employee at a pharmaceutical firm who did not receive the promotion he desired but instead was given constructive feedback by his employer on how he could improve his performance. His mother called the human resources department 17 times; she demanded a mediation session with her, her son, his boss, and the human resources representative—and she got it!

Career centers on college campuses are offering more resources to help parents support their children in the process of finding internships and careers (Keppler, Mullendore, & Carey, 2005; Lehman, 2005). For example, the Career Services Office at the University of Nevada–Las Vegas (UNLV) provides guidelines on its Web site for parents who are helping their children through the career development process. The information on the Web site is organized by college year and details the roles of students, parents, and career services employees; it advises parents to direct communications to their children rather than to potential employers. For example, parents of juniors are advised to "talk with your son or daughter about career goals and plans for after graduation and utilizing the resources in their Career Services Office" (UNLV, 2006).

SUMMARY

Through leadership development, career centers, academic course-work, and other means, institutions of higher education are reconsidering how to support and challenge members of the Net Generation to provide them with the best opportunities and preparation for postgraduate life. This generation is presenting a challenge to employers, who have worked more easily with previous generations of employees.

RECOMMENDATIONS

In 2004, the first wave of Net Gen students graduated from college and faced the transition to a multigenerational workforce. In college, they expected and received many adjustments from their institutions adapting to their culture; the world of work is not so accommodating. Net Gen students are relatively unprepared for the work environment that has been molded by the Silent Generation, Boomers, and Gen Xers. Career services profession-als must work with these students to help them in their career searches and help them learn the skills they will need to be effective in the workplace. Recommendations for this effort include the following:

> Career services professionals need to understand the work values of Net Generation students and educate these stu-dents about expectations of the multigenerational workforce to help them make the transition to the world of work.

☐ Advisors should review procedures for working with re-cruiters. For instance, it is important for Net Generation students to understand that employers expect them to follow through on an employment commitment and not decline a job because they have received other offers.

☐ Employers should capitalize on the strengths of Net Generation employees, especially their multitasking capabilities, technological skills, and ability to work well in groups. At the same time, Net Gen employees can capitalize on their abilities to interact in teams to reach their goals.

REFERENCES

Alberta Learning Information Service Web site. (2005). Bridging the generation gap at work. Retrieved September 29, 2006, from http://www.alis. gov.ab.ca/tips/archive.asp?EK=7380

Alsop, R. (2006, February 14). Millennial M.B.A.s prompt a shift in approach, services at schools. Retrieved January 25, 2007, from http://www.career-journal.com/columnists/mbatrack/20060214-alsop.html

Armour, S. (2005, November 7). Generation Y: They've arrived at work with a new attitude. *USA Today*, p. C1.

Center for Generational Studies. (2005). Frequently asked questions about generational differences. Retrieved July 25, 2006, from http://www. gentrends.com/faq.html

Coomes, M. D., & DeBard, R. (2004). A generational approach to understanding students. In M. D. Coomes & R. DeBard (Eds.), *Serving the millennial generation: New directions for student services, no. 106* (pp. 5–16). San Francisco: Jossey-Bass.

DeBard, R. (2004). Millennials coming to college. In M. D. Coomes & R. DeBard (Eds.), *Serving the millennial generation: New directions for student services, no. 106* (pp. 33–45). San Francisco: Jossey-Bass.

ePolicy Institute. (2004). 2004 workplace e-mail and instant messaging survey. Retrieved November 10, 2006, from http://www.epolicyinstitute. com/survey/survey04.pdf

Eubanks, M. R. (2006, October 4). Millennial generation has fresh ideas, expects more from job. *Times Daily.* Retrieved October 29, 2006, from http://www.ledger-enquirer.com/mld/ledgerenquirer/news/ local/15677178.htm

Gerdes, L. (2006, September 16). The best places to launch a career. Business Week Online. Retrieved November 7, 2006, from http://www. businessweek.com

Green, E. (2006, June 12). Work zone: New grads seek jobs focusing on fun, ethics, and social worth. *Pittsburgh Post-Gazette.* Retrieved July 25, 2006, from http://www.post-gazette.com/pg/pp/060163/697149.stm

Howe, N., & Strauss, W. (2000). *Millennials rising: The next great generation.* New York: Vintage Books.

Jayson, S. (2006, June 29). The 'millennials' come of age. *USA Today*, p. D1.

Junco, R. (2005). Technology and today's first-year students. In M. L. Upcraft, J. N. Gardner, B. O. Barefoot, & associates (Eds.), *Meeting challenges and building support: Creating a climate for first-year student success* (pp 221–238). San Francisco: Jossey-Bass.

Keppler, K., Mullendore, R. H., & Carey, A. (2005). *Partnering with the parents of today's college students.* Washington, DC: National Association of Student Personnel Administrators.

Lancaster, L. C., & Stillman, D. (2002). *When generations collide.* New York: Harper Collins.

Lehman, G. (2005, November 20). Parents are encouraged to interact, not overreact. *Miami Herald*, p. 3EG.

Lowery, J. W. (2004) Student affairs for a new generation. In M. D. Coomes & R. DeBard (Eds.), *Serving the millennial generation: New directions for student services, no.106* (pp. 87–99) San Francisco: Jossey-Bass.

Margulius, D. L. (2006). Telecommuting gets more elusive. *InfoWorld, 28*(6), 18

NAS Recruitment Communications. (2006). Generation Y: The millennials – ready or not, here they come. Retrieved July 27, 2006, from http://www.nasrecruitment.com/TalentTips/NASinsights/GenerationY.pdf

Rainie, L. (2006, September 28). Digital 'natives' invade the workplace. Pew Internet and American Life Project. Retrieved January 28, 2007, from http://pewresearch.org/pubs/70/digital-natives-invade-the-workplace

121

Raines, C. (2002). Managing millennials. Retrieved November 8, 2006, from http://www.generationsatwork.com/articles/millenials.htm

Reesor, L., & Schlabach, K. (2006, Fall). Managing multi-generations: Strategies for crossing the generational divide in the workplace. *Leadership Exchange, 4*(3), 16–19.

Sacks, D. (2006, January). Scenes from the culture clash. *Fast Company, 102,* 72.

Shiu, E., & Lenhart, A. (2004). *How Americans use instant messaging.* Washington, DC: Pew Internet and American Life Project.

University of Nevada-Las Vegas Career Services. (2006). Information for parents. Retrieved July 25, 2006, from http://hire.unlv.edu/parents/parents.htm

Universum Communications. (2006). The American undergraduate edition. Retrieved July 29, 2006, from http://www.universumusa.com/undergraduate.html

Zemke, R., Raines, C., & Filipczak, B. (2000). *Generations at work: Managing the clash of Veterans, Boomers, Xers, and Nexters in your workplace.* New York: American Management Association.

Zetter, K. & Albro, E. N. (2006, October). Employers crack down on personal Net use. *PC World, 24*(10), 26–26.

Chapter 7

Academic Advising with the Net Generation

Academic advising is one of the most important ways that college students, especially first-year students, connect with campus representatives (King & Kerr, 2005). Academic advisors facilitate students' learning and help them with educational, career, and personal decision making in the context of each student's values, interests, and abilities (Grites & Gordon, 2000; King & Kerr, 2005). In this chapter, we review information about advising Net Generation students. We discuss how technology has influenced the delivery of advising and address workplace issues related to Net Generation students.

Net Generation students are traditional-aged students in the early stages of adult development. Accordingly, in their work with Net Gen students, academic advisors typically apply the ideas of challenging and supporting young adults who are moving through identity development (Chickering & Reisser, 1993; Strange, 2004). Advising these college students presents unique challenges because their parents are highly involved in their college experiences and because the Net Generation is a pressured, achieving, and sheltered generation. Strange (2004) suggested that the Net Generation's focus on collaboration may reorder the importance of independence in their development, and may signal regression and immaturity.

Keeling (2003) said that an effective academic advisor is aware of generational trends and patterns. Information about how to best serve Net Generation advisees is an important component of professional development as academic advisors constantly improve their methods of serving and assisting students. Recent conferences related to academic advising—including the October 2005 annual meeting of the National Academic Advising Association (NACADA)—have hosted sessions on trends in working with Net Generation students.

NET GENERATION STUDENTS AND ADVISING

Net Generation students' expectations present a challenge for academic advisors (Keeling, 2003). Schneider and Stevenson (1999) concluded that Net Generation teenagers have ambitions but no realistic plans (see also Keeling, 2003). Many Net Gen students have undefined career and academic goals when they arrive at college; they "have limited knowledge about their chosen occupations, about educational requirements, or about future demand for those occupations" (Schneider & Stevenson, 1999, p. 7). Schneider and Stevenson discussed the results of the Alfred P. Sloan Study of Youth and Social Development, which showed that 56.2% of the adolescents surveyed were "expecting to obtain either more or less education than the average person who works in their desired occupation" (p. 81).

Keeling (2003) recommended that advisors guide students by asking direct questions such as, "Why do you want to major in [intended major]?" and, "What is it about [intended career] that interests you?" to help them match their ambitions to their expectations. The influence of parents in their goal-setting and their comfort with being given direction by authority figures can mean that these students have difficulty making decisions and lack some critical thinking skills. Often students who are undecided about their majors need assistance with the decision-making process, and it is recommended that advisors use interest inventories with current information on career theory and research to help them with career choices (Keeling, 2003).

Howe and Strauss (2000) described the pressured Net Generation students as perceiving that "everything they want in life is critically dependent upon their own performance" (p. 184). The college admissions process has been a primary focus for this generation. Students spend their K–12 years building portfolios of grades and extracurricular activities to compete with their peers (Trudeau, 2006). In college, instead of setting new kinds of goals, these students continue with the behavior they know. Schneider and Stevenson (1999) observed that college students lack the skills to set and reach goals; their experience has been limited to getting into college. So they continue to assemble the best portfolios they can of grades and extracurricular activities. They may not be able to articulate what the portfolios are for, but they want to make sure that they have strong ones compared with their peers. Net Generation students frequently want to know in advance how prospective graduate schools and employers will judge the decisions they make. For example, students are often afraid to drop courses because withdrawals will be noted on their transcripts and they worry that this will have negative consequences (sometimes missing the point that failing grades will have worse consequences).

The diversity of today's college students means that advisors must understand minority populations and address their needs (Keeling, 2003; King & Kerr, 2005). Since advisors are a primary source of referrals to other campus resources, they should have a solid knowledge base concerning the issues that typically face various student populations and the appropriate resources to deal with these issues (King & Kerr, 2005).

One example of students with unique needs is students with disabilities. The percentage of college students with disabilities has increased in the past two decades and continues to grow (Frieden, 2003; Wilson, 2004), and academic advisors are often primary sources of referrals for students who have not yet been tested for disabilities. A large number of students are diagnosed with learning disabilities during college (Frieden, 2003; Wilson, 2004); it is often the academic advisor who recognizes a pattern of poor academic performance (e.g., difficulty passing math courses) and recommends that the student be tested for learning disabilities.

Other common referrals made by academic advisors are for counseling and psychological needs, which are increasing among Net Generation students (American College Health Association, 2006; Lowery, 2004). Academic advisors are frequently students' primary sources of contact with the institution; often, they meet with a student to talk about academic problems and discover that the problems are actually psychological.

TECHNOLOGY AND ACADEMIC ADVISING

Because the Net Generation is using technology at vastly higher rates than members of other generations, academic advisors have adopted electronic communication technologies to help them connect with their students (Steele & Carter, 2002). Multari (2004) wrote, "Today's students are twenty-four-hour, seven-day-a-week customers who reject the disadvantages of traditional nine to five administrative practices. Technology provides extended access to information, interaction, and client-centered

126

applications." Steele and Carter (2002) pointed out, "Most [academic advisors] are drowning in incoming e-mail messages with overflowing inboxes and blinking lights on our voice mail. Responding effectively to student inquires requires an integrated, managed use of these technologies." Academic advisors at large institutions typically receive up to 150 e-mails a day from students asking general academic advising questions. Often the answers are available in the institution's catalog or in a list of frequently asked questions, but members of the Net Generation prefer to ask questions rather than search for answers.

Consistent information is a necessary and important part of good academic advising, even when the message is repetitive and is published in several locations (Steele & Carter, 2002). Academic advising is often a rehashing of institutional policies as they apply to a specific student; often, students either do not seek answers before meeting with advisors or are hoping for exceptions to the policies. Before technology provided additional options, advisors used various means to disseminate answers to commonly asked questions about curricula, course registration, policies and procedures, and to offer general advice (Steele & Carter, 2002). In the past, fliers in residence halls, postings on campus bulletin boards, and general announcements in classes and the student newspaper were the most common methods of sharing information. Advisors can use technology to increase both the efficiency and effectiveness of their work (King & Kerr, 2005).

The delivery of academic advising online will increase the use of virtual contacts with students and is not restrained by office hours or staff availability during the day (Multari, 2004). Historically, academic advising has followed the classic work day of 8 a.m. to 5 p.m.; however, today's advisors must reach out to serve students at their preferred times and locations. The University of Central Florida, for example, sets up booths during peak registration times in areas that students frequent. Academic advising in the residence halls has expanded to meet students where they live, and evening advising reaches them during their preferred hours. The challenge for advisors is to balance the use of technology with human resources (Multari, 2004).

King and Kerr (2005) list several ways of advising students using technology: synchronous advising (real-time advising in which the advisor and advisee are in different locations—this can be achieved over the phone or Internet); videoconferencing; computer chats and Voice Over Internet Protocol (VOIP) audio conferencing (participants talk over the Internet simultaneously); structural delivery systems (such as TVs, radios, satellites, and CD-ROMs); and asynchronous advising (includes e-mail, video mail, and voice mail). For example, Clemson University uses webcams to provide academic advising to students (Cawthon, Havice, & Havice, 2003). And as the technology has become more commonplace, universities have included chat functions for students on campus, off campus, and in distance education programs. LaGuardia Community College provides virtual interest groups in the form of asynchronous, five-week advising seminars attached to various learning communities and key courses; this is especially useful for the college's commuting, working, and increasingly part-time student body (Lucca & Arcario, 2006).

Net Generation Parents

As noted in previous chapters, the parents of today's students expect to be fully integrated into their children's college experience. Advisors typically have challenged and supported college students as they moved toward autonomy and independence; now these advisors "must adopt a new approach to advising that will still create an environment for students to realize their autonomy and develop an educational plan consistent with their personal goals" (Menezes, 2005).

Net Generation parents want to ensure that their children have every possible advantage—parents work hard to provide private tutors and college-selection counselors, and do not hesitate to advocate for their children in college admissions processes and anywhere else if they perceive a lack of fairness (Keeling, 2003). There is a widening gap between those who can afford college and those who cannot (Selingo & Brainard, 2006), and the parents who are most involved in their college students' lives tend to be more affluent and have more resources.

An example of a recent incident at a public university demonstrates the growing trend of parental advocacy. A parent blamed the institution for the student's failure to complete the foreign language graduation requirement, despite several meetings between the student and his advisors during which the student was informed of the steps he needed to take to graduate (Mastrodicasa & Kepic, 2005). Despite the fact that the student did not complete the requirements, he attempted to matriculate in graduate school at another institution; he was turned down because of his lack of a bachelor's degree. The student's father e-mailed the university president, the director of the academic advising center, the dean of the college, and the governor of the state; he accused the institution of not taking enough responsibility to resolve his son's dilemma. The situation was eventually resolved by having the student complete the required courses because the advisors had carefully documented the content of advising sessions and placed this information in the student's file (Mastrodicasa & Kepic, 2005).

129

Net Generation students' willingness to listen to authority figures also affects academic advising. Because they participated in organized activities throughout their youth, these students are likely to count on and trust authority (DeBard, 2004). In fact, students often have difficulty choosing course electives beyond requirements, because they have not had many opportunities to make such choices. Approximately two thirds of states require high school exit exams; in many cases, accountability testing in numerous subjects has reduced or precluded elective choices at the high school level (Center on Education Policy, 2006). Net Generation students' tremendous focus on putting together solid high school portfolios of the "right" courses makes it hard for them to select college classes that might be interesting or fun.

SHIFTS IN THE ADVISING WORKPLACE

In higher education, Boomers make up the majority of senior faculty and advising administrators, while Gen Xers serve as frontline advisors and are moving into administrative positions (Gordon & Steele, 2005). Advisors from the Net Generation are most likely new hires or graduate students. Gordon and Steele (2005) recommend appreciation for and sensitivity toward the values, experiences, and perceptions of each generation as a way to keep the advising workplace productive. Also, it is important to recognize that Net Generation students plan to have several careers in various work settings; in fact, this is true of Net Generation academic advisors as well (Gordon & Steele, 2005).

Net Generation advisors tend to be multitaskers and prefer to use good manners and formality in their daily contacts. With a focus on authenticity and accuracy, the Net Generation advisors are goal-oriented (Gordon & Steele, 2005). They have "a distaste for menial work, are sometimes impatient, and lack skills for dealing with difficult people" (Raines, 2003, p. 182). Like college students, Net Generation advisors are energized, high-achieving people who do not consider differences in race, ethnicity, and gender to be important (Gordon & Steele, 2005; Leo, 2003). Rather, they value multiculturalism and diversity in the workplace (Gordon & Steele, 2005).

SUMMARY

Students often make initial and ongoing contact with their institutions of higher education through their academic advisors. This generation of students presents advisors with new challenges, including the role of parents in students' lives and the need to help students make realistic plans to reach their goals. It is more important than ever for academic advisors to stay up-to-date on the constantly evolving technology trends in the profession. The delivery of academic advising services can only improve as students and advisors rely on new forms of technology as communication tools. Academic advisors should look to their colleagues and associations for professional development opportunities.

RECOMMENDATIONS

📂 Because advisors have a great deal of contact with students, it is important that they recognize indicators of disabilities and psychological disorders and make appropriate referrals to disability services and counseling centers.

📂 As research (e.g., Junco, in preparation) has shown, Net Generation students do not have a solid understanding of the advisor and advisee roles and responsibilities. These students are comfortable with authority and order, so it is feasible to educate them about what they should expect from the advising process. It is appropriate for advisors to ask students to come to meetings with ideas about courses they may want to take and to do "homework" regarding their desired majors and career paths.

📂 In the case of chronically undecided students, advisors may need to become directive and suggest courses that fit with the preferences students express, even if dispensing such advice goes against the advisor's own style. Students' preferences can be ascertained through career development inventories as well as direct, guided questioning.

📂 Advisors can be particularly helpful to their students when they use technology to communicate with them in creative

131

ways. The use of instant messaging programs for "drop-in" advising has been very successful, especially for advisees who are more introverted and less likely to stop by to speak with advisors. Another modality that will reach Net Generation students is having advisors moderate discussions in chat rooms and on blogs.

☐ Net Generation students expect immediate service and around-the-clock access to faculty and staff; yet they sometimes find it difficult to make appointments to see advisors. Installing advising stations in popular campus locations gives students opportunities to ask questions and obtain accurate information.

☐ It is important to provide consistently accurate information in all the different modalities. Advising information should be easily accessible from the college or university's main Web page and in print publications, and should be communicated effectively to faculty who advise students.

☐ Creating publications for parents that outline student and advisor responsibilities is helpful to head off parental perceptions that advisors are not doing the right thing.

REFERENCES

American College Health Association. (2006). National College Health Assessment Web Summary. Retrieved October 4, 2006, from http://www. acha.org/projects_programs/ncha_sampledata.cfm

Cawthon, T. W., Havice, P. A., & Havice, W. L. (2003). Enhancing collaboration in student affairs: Virtual advising. *Student Affairs Online, 4*(4). Retrieved August 11, 2006, from http://studentaffairs.com/ejournal/Fall_ 2003/Virtualadvising.html

Center on Education Policy. (2006, August). State high school exit exams: A challenging year. Retrieved November 7, 2006, from http://www.cep-dc.org/pubs/hseeAugust2006

Chickering, A. W., & Reisser. L. (1993). *Education and identity* (2nd ed.). San Francisco: Jossey-Bass.

DeBard, R. (2004). Millennials coming to college. In M. D. Coomes & R. DeBard (Eds.), *Serving the millennial generation: New directions for student services, no. 106* (pp. 33–45). San Francisco: Jossey-Bass.

Frieden, L. (2003, September 15). *People with disabilities and postsecondary education*. Washington, DC: National Council on Disability. Retrieved August 11, 2006, from http://www.ncd.gov/newsroom/publications/2003/education.htm

Gordon, V. N., & Steele, M. J. (2005). The advising workplace: Generational differences and challenges. *NACADA Journal, 25*(1), 26–30.

Grites, T., & Gordon, V. (2000). Developmental academic advising revisited. *NACADA Journal, 20*(1), 12–15.

Howe, N., & Strauss, W. (2000). *Millennials rising: The next great generation*. New York: Vintage Books.

Junco, R. (in preparation). Psychometric properties of an online advisor evaluation instrument.

Keeling, S. (2003). Advising the millennial generation. *NACADA Journal, 23*(1–2), 30–36.

King, M. C., & Kerr, T. J. (2005). Academic advising. In M. L. Upcraft, J. N. Gardner, & B. O. Barefoot (Eds.), *Challenging and supporting the first-year student: A handbook for improving the first year of college* (pp. 320–338). San Francisco: Jossey-Bass.

Leo, J. (2003, November 3). The good-news generation. *U.S. News and World Report.* Retrieved January 25, 2007, from http://www.usnews.com/usnews/opinion/articles/031103/3john.htm

Lowery, J. W. (2004). Student affairs for a new generation. In M. D. Coomes & R. DeBard (Eds.), *Serving the millennial generation: New directions for student services, no. 106* (pp. 87–99). San Francisco: Jossey-Bass.

Lucca, L., & Arcario, P. (2006). Online advising through virtual interest groups. *The Mentor: An Academic Advisement Journal.* Retrieved November 7, 2006, from http://www.psu.edu/dus/mentor

Mastrodicasa, J. M., & Kepic, G. (2005, October). *Parents gone wild.* Paper presented at meeting of National Academic Advising Association, Las Vegas, NV.

Menezes, M. D. (2005). Advisors and parents: Together building stronger advising relationships. Retrieved July 5, 2006, from http://www.nacada.ksu.edu/Clearinghouse/AdvisingIssues/Advisors-Parents.htm

Multari, R. J. (2004). Technology in higher education academic advisement. *The Mentor: An Academic Advisement Journal.* Retrieved July 7, 2006, from http://www.psu.edu/dus/mentor/040107rm.htm

Raines, C. (2003). *Connecting generations: The sourcebook for a new workplace.* Menlo Park, CA: Crisp Publications.

Schneider, B., & Stevenson, D. (1999). *The ambitious generation: America's teenagers, motivated but directionless.* New Haven, CT: Yale University Press.

Selingo, J., & Brainard, J. (2006, April 7). The rich-poor gap widens for colleges and students. *Chronicle of Higher Education, 42*(31), A1.

Steele, G., & Carter, A. (2002, December). Managing electronic communication technologies for more effective advising. *Academic Advising News, 25*(4). Retrieved July 7, 2006, from http://www.nacada.ksu.edu/Clearinghouse/AdvisingIssues/electronic.htm

Strange, C. C. (2004). Constructions of student development across the generations. In M. D. Coomes & R. DeBard (Eds.), *Serving the millennial generation: New directions for student services, no. 106* (47–57). San Francisco: Jossey-Bass.

Trudeau, M. (2006, October 9). School, study, SATs: No wonder teens are stressed. Morning Edition, National Public Radio. Retrieved November 7, 2006, from http://www.npr.org/templates/story/story.php?storyId=6221 872&sc=emaf

Wilson, M. E. (2004). Teaching, learning, and millennial students. In M. D. Coomes & R. DeBard (Eds.), *Serving the millennial generation: New directions for student services, no. 106* (pp. 59–71). San Francisco: Jossey-Bass.

Chapter 8

Pedagogy with the Net Generation

N et Generation students are unique in their psychosocial makeup, as discussed in previous chapters. They are also unique in how they learn and how they experience the college classroom. The classroom is another place in which the differences between the Net Generation and previous generations are greatly illuminated. As in the workplace, members of different generations (Net Gen students and their pre-Net Gen faculty) sometimes misunderstand each other in the classroom. Numerous faculty members have commented to the authors that they think their Net Gen students are aloof and unwilling to focus in class. In reality, Net Gen students genuinely attempt to be engaged and sometimes have difficulty doing so in environments that do not match their online world in terms of speed and communication styles. In this chapter, we review the learning styles of the Net Generation and ways to reach them with different teaching techniques.

Faculty members today are much more advanced in their teaching strategies than ever before. They are generally well-versed in learning theories and techniques that help pre-Net Gen students learn. They are also familiar with the use of technology in teaching, using tools such as PowerPoint slides, SmartBoard hardware and software, and Clicker real-time response devices. While faculty members are aware of learning theories, they are less familiar with the latest research on how Net Generation students process information, learn best, and communicate their knowledge (Ramaley & Zia, 2006). And the fact that faculty use technology in their courses does not ensure that Net Generation students will feel engaged in the classroom (Hartman, Moskal, & Dziuban, 2006).

NET GENERATION CHARACTERISTICS

Net Generation students share a combination of qualities that tend to surprise people from other generations. While these characteristics can be found in individuals from all generations, the combination and the fact that the previous generation (Generation X) exhibited the opposite characteristics surprises many people. Net Generation learners are:

- Driven

- Social

- Experiential learners

- Multitaskers

Driven

Net Generation students place intense pressure on themselves to succeed, and they believe that short-term achievement determines long-term success. Students from this generation have very scheduled lives and feel pressured to get into the "right" colleges. The Net Generation is goal-oriented, yet its members lack the skills needed to prevent burnout and manage their time (Lowery, 2004). In high school, these students know that obtaining top grades will not by itself get them into the colleges of their choice, so they create portfolios that show them as well-rounded persons. This self-imposed pressure, combined with their achieving nature, makes Net Generation students one of the most stressed groups to show up on college campuses to date. Indeed, the percentage of college students who reported experiencing depression or anxiety in the previous year has increased dramatically since 2000 (American College Health Association, 2006). Recent data from the ACHA National College Health Assessment (NCHA) show that 36% of female and 45% of male students reported being so depressed at some point over the previous year that it was difficult for them to function (American College Health Association, 2006).

Members of the Net Generation may catch faculty off guard with their driven nature and strong commitment to their own success. Faculty report that today's students challenge their grades at much higher rates than students in the past. Net Generation students sometimes demand to know why their grades were A-minuses and not A's, and they have been known to ask for higher grades because they need to keep their GPAs at certain levels. This generation of students prefers objective methods of evaluation over subjective ones (Lowery, 2004). They want to know exactly what they have to do to earn A's; and they request explicit syllabi and well-structured assignments that provide clear expectations (Wilson, 2004).

On some occasions, their parents call faculty and student affairs staff to inquire or argue about grades (Lowery, 2004). Actively involved parents are engaged in other aspects of their Net Generation students' academic lives as well, such as choosing their courses or majors, monitoring course content on controversial issues, and attending hearings regarding academic dishonesty (Wilson, 2004). Faculty members from other generations often consider this behavior inappropriate and insulting. Most professors went through college understanding that they had to be their own advocates and that, ultimately, decisions about grades were in the faculty domain. Conversations suggesting that faculty members had made mistakes in grading were either avoided or conducted with a great deal of tact. Today, when grades are posted, Net Generation students can quickly write e-mail messages demanding explanations and challenging their grades. Instructors receive numerous e-mails from students (rather than phone calls or visits) about grades, and in some cases the tone of these e-mails can be offensive.

Another consequence of the Net Generation students' drive is that they (possibly unknowingly) forgo development of their critical thinking skills. They tend to think that short-term achievement equals long-term success; therefore, they focus on grades and not on the processes by which grades are obtained. Typical Net Generation students are not interested in how they arrived at the correct conclusions as long as they receive full credit for their answers. Both authors have had personal conversations in which Net Gen students reveal that they give professors "the answers they want to hear" rather than students' own opinions or ideas. These same students sometimes later express their frustration to family and friends about not being able to be straightforward because they fear reprisal in the form of lower grades.

Ironically, this phenomenon may be a contributing factor to the involvement of ultraconservative political groups in trying to censor professors who espouse liberal ideologies. Instead of confronting the professors directly—which Net Gen students think might hurt their grades—they complain to their parents. Outraged by such "indoctrination" and predisposed to protect their children, the parents pressure legislators to support censorship laws (Lipka, 2005). Legislation that attempts to limit faculty academic freedom (such as the Academic Bill of Rights) has been introduced in a number of states, and some of these laws have passed or universities have voluntarily adopted the legislators' suggestions.

There has not necessarily been an increase in professors espousing leftist ideas; the difference is that students from previous generations would have confronted the faculty members directly in the classroom or through campus complaint procedures (which involve progressively higher levels of authority in university governance). Net Gen students feel less able to be straightforward and confrontational with faculty because of the great pressure they put on themselves to get good grades (Strauss & Howe, 2006).

Social

Net Generation students are social and team-oriented. They have worked on school assignments in groups, including joint presentations that resulted in a collective grade, and have participated on teams their entire lives. They prefer social interaction in their learning; that is, they like to interact with professors and peers and value the development of meaningful relationships with them (McNeely, 2006; Oblinger & Oblinger, 2006; Roberts, 2006; Windham, 2006). Research has shown that learning is enhanced by using interactive activities both in and out of the classroom (Kuh, 2003). Wilson (2004) suggested that active learning for this generation requires fewer lectures and more discussions, cooperative learning, and group projects. Faculty can include student interaction in the design of courses—creating study groups, learning partners, and other connections among students.

141

Experiential Learners

Net Gen students also learn very well through experiential learning—knowledge that is organized by the learner and obtained through direct participation or experience. Net Gen students have used computers throughout their academic development. The Pew Internet and American

Life Project reported that 20% of students started using computers between the ages of 5 and 8 years (Jones, 2002). More recent national data show that 21% of children 2 years and younger, 58% of 3- to 4-year-olds, and 77% of 5- to 6-year-olds have used computers (Calvert, Rideout, Woolard, Barr, & Strouse, 2005). One outcome of extensive computer use is a great deal of experience with trial-and-error learning—Net Generation students intuitively know how to solve technology problems, because they have learned this way their entire lives. In conversations with the authors, Net Gen students have said that they rarely read instruction manuals; in fact, manufacturers of appliances, gadgets, and electronics have started including "quick start" guides for these consumers.

Net Generation students want to reach their own conclusions about material presented in class. They are accustomed to exploring the Internet to obtain information and, therefore, like to engage in this same process in their real-world learning. Instead of being told about the social and economic causes of the Civil War, they would rather read original records of the Union and Confederate states in the Valley of the Shadows archive and arrive at their own conclusions (Oblinger & Oblinger, 2006).

142

One of the authors (Junco) has found that to teach students how to find legitimate articles on the Internet, he needs to reduce his lecture time and increase the interactivity of the process. He briefly introduces an assignment in which students are to find "bogus" and "legitimate" research articles. He gives basic guidance and then lets the students search for articles and bring them back to class for discussion. Over the years, this approach has worked much better than two or three sessions of explaining the differences among peer-reviewed journals, self-published research, and conjecture.

Multitaskers

Net Generation students are prolific multitaskers—they easily juggle a number of tasks that require cognitive resources. In fact, these students are not just adept at multitasking; they actually work best when they are multitasking. Data from the Net Generation Survey (see chapter 4) show that 75% of IM users did schoolwork while instant messaging; 91.9% engaged in other activities on their computers while instant messaging; and 75.1% engaged in non-computer-related activities, such as watching TV or talking on the phone. Even though most Net Generation students function best when multitasking, a subsample of this population may suffer negative consequences from Internet use. On the Net Generation Survey, 40.2% of students reported that surfing the Web hurt their schoolwork while only 28% reported that their schoolwork was hurt by instant messaging. These data are in agreement with Junco's (2005) assertion that the use of the Internet for noncommunication purposes affects students' psychological well-being more than use of the Internet to communicate.

The idea that students are multitasking while working on class assignments makes faculty members shudder. Generally, faculty do not believe that students can divide their attention among multiple tasks and retain course material. However, Net Generation students—partly because of their familiarity with computing technology and the development of their learning processes using such technology—have developed cognitive processing styles that can be described as "hypertext" in nature. Their attention skips around from point to point, as when a person is using the Internet and following hyperlinks in no linear order. Being raised in a digital age has caused a shift in thinking from linear to nonlinear. Gen Xers and earlier generations arrived at knowledge through linear thinking, which was a by-product of the technology available at the time (largely print media). It is entirely possible that Net Generation students' brains have developed morphological and physiological changes to adapt to the different needs of their environments (Prensky, 2001).

Whether or not these cerebral changes have occurred, it is clear that the capacity for multitasking and hypertext modes of thinking is ingrained in Net Gen students through early exposure to nonlinear environments.

143

These students intuitively solve technology problems, multitask, and arrive at knowledge in their own way. Net Gen students have shorter attention spans than people from previous generations (Prensky, 2001). Again, the technology they use drives their cognitive processes. Why send a whole e-mail message when you can just text-message the main point? In educational terms, why listen to a whole lecture when you can figure out the main point on your own?

TEACHING STRATEGIES

Wilson (2004) and Kuh (2003) reviewed several strategies for effective teaching for all students, with a focus on the Net Generation. Student-faculty contact has always been considered an important part of the learning process, but it is the quality, not the quantity, of the contact that matters—extensive contact is not necessary. Student-faculty contacts that encourage students to seek educationally purposeful activities during college—such as discussing career plans or research projects, receiving prompt feedback, discussing course requirements or grades, or even talking about ideas outside of class—are all part of active learning. It is often the more successful students who seek these kinds of interactions, but faculty should attempt to learn the names of all students and seek informal contact with them (Kuh, 2003; Wilson, 2004).

Activities that engage and involve students are considered to be the optimal methods of promoting active student learning, especially compared with the passive lecture-discussion format (Wilson, 2004). The team-oriented nature of the Net Generation makes these activities even more desirable for current students. Students learn better when they engage with the material, relate it to their own experience, and apply it to their lives than they do by memorizing information, listening to lectures, and repeating information back on tests (Chickering & Gamson, 1987; Wilson, 2004).

It is important for Net Generation students to feel connected to their instructors. Long and Coldren (2006) found that Net Generation students can be engaged even in large, lecture-based courses. They discovered that faculty who teach by using personal examples, showing students how to do things, and encouraging teamwork were considered most effective by Net Gen students. Long and Coldren (2006) provided specific examples of ways faculty can increase their connections with students:

- Explain your thinking, not just your answers.

- Laugh at your mistakes and use them as opportunities for learning. The students will see professors as problem solvers and will learn how they detect and correct errors in thinking.

- Create a team atmosphere. Refer to "we" when addressing your class to connote a sense of shared responsibility.

- Use personal anecdotes, but make them professionally relevant.

- Use engaging nonverbal cues.

- Talk to, not at, your students. Try to establish a conversational atmosphere.

- Get excited. If you want your students to be excited about learning, you as the instructor have to be excited about teaching the material (pp. 241–242).

Another way for faculty to engage students is to make an effort to understand their backgrounds. Learning about the shared characteristics of Net Generation students is one way to understand their experiences. Or, for example, it can be helpful to know whether most students are the first in their families to go to college or whether they all come from the same geographic region. Students will sense the personal interest in them; this translates into more positive ratings for the faculty member and better educational outcomes for the student (Long & Coldren, 2006).

Students from the Net Generation tend to not spend enough time on any task, particularly studying. Members of this generation expect high levels of achievement but do not put in the time necessary to earn high grades (Wilson, 2004). Grade inflation at the high school and college levels is well documented, giving students a false sense of achievement (Lowery, 2004; Wilson, 2004). The amount of studying by college students is typically much lower than what is recommended—two hours outside of class for each hour in class (Pryor, Hurtado, Saenz, Lindholm, Korn, & Mahoney, 2005). Overall, there is a disconnect between Net Generation students' goals and efforts—and yet, they are confident and motivated to achieve (Wilson, 2004).

TECHNOLOGY AND THE CLASSROOM

Throughout their secondary schooling and into college, Net Gen students have been required to use programs such as Microsoft PowerPoint for presentations, Excel to create spreadsheets, and Word to type their papers. Net Generation students started using computers at very early ages, and they spend a great deal of time using them. A recent report by the Kaiser Family Foundation (2005) found that children ages 8 to 18 years spend more time using computers and playing video games than reading; on average, children spend about an hour a day using computers and about 45 minutes each playing video games and reading. Net Generation Survey data show that college students typically spend almost an hour and a half a day chatting on IM, log on to Facebook twice a day, and spend an hour a week reading blogs (see chapter 4).

Net Generation students expect faculty members to incorporate technology into their teaching and to be proficient at it (Wilson, 2004). Faculty members sometimes use "course shells" to supplement class instruction.

Course shells (such as WebCT and Blackboard) add an online component to the class; they include moderated discussions, chat rooms, and testing engines where faculty can set up exams and students can log on to take exams at predetermined times. The moderated discussions and chats allow professors to engage students in ways that are not possible in nonvirtual classrooms, and these formats encourage more introverted students to communicate their ideas through a modality that is less stressful and more familiar to them. Course shells also offer around-the-clock access to syllabi, assignments, course news, and frequently asked questions.

While course shells supplement classes, online courses are completely encapsulated Web-based courses. The first Web-based courses were geared toward distance education students; recently, campus-based students have been allowed and even encouraged to take Web-based courses to meet their degree requirements. Online courses have not yet delivered on their potential as a catalyst to transform the traditional learning process. Net Generation students do not particularly like courses that are entirely online (Windham, 2006), primarily because of the lack of engagement and interaction. Since Net Generation students embrace interaction and are focused on achievement, online courses often turn into mere searches for information to complete assignments and get good grades.

Interaction with professors is crucial for Net Generation students. Wilson (2004) recommended methods for faculty to connect with students in online courses, including creating opportunities for chats, posting biographies of instructors, and scheduling opportunities for personal interaction, such as a class trip. Certainly, many nuances inherent in human interaction cannot be mimicked in online mediums. For instance, we can usually tell in a face-to-face interaction if we've said something offensive or upsetting. The other person's body language, facial expressions, tone, and energy level are apparent in the real-world situation. Reading these cues is nearly impossible in an online medium. Research shows that it is very difficult to ascertain the intended tone of an e-mail message and that people think they can communicate tone in e-mail more effectively than they actually do (Epley & Kruger, 2004; Kruger, Epley, Parker, & Ng, 2005).

Another concern for faculty members is the expansion of the cut-and-paste mind-set. While the Web makes it easier for Net Gen students to perform research, it also makes it easier for them to plagiarize information from Web sites. In a nationwide survey, the Center for Academic Integrity (2005) found that 40% of college students reported engaging in cut-and-paste plagiarism and 77% reported that they did not think that cut-and-paste plagiarism is a very serious issue. Nelson Laird and Kuh (2005) found that 87% of students in their sample reported that their classmates cut-and-paste information from the Internet without citing a source. Because of the vast numbers of Web sites and the expanding nature of the Web, it can be very difficult or even impossible to catch these instances of plagiarism. Companies such as TurnItIn.com offer plagiarism-checking services to universities on a subscription basis. A student must upload a paper to the checking Web site, which compares it against Web databases and databases of papers turned in by other students at other universities. The service then sends faculty members an "originality report" and an "originality score" for the paper.

Addressing plagiarism among Net Generation students requires a different approach than that used with previous generations (Langlais, 2006). The fact that 77% of students said they did not think cut-and-paste plagiarism was a serious infraction indicates that these students need more education about the issue (Center for Academic Integrity, 2005). And because much of the plagiarism engaged in by Net Generation students involves technology, it is important that faculty learn corresponding techniques to discover and contend with plagiarism. Faculty members who want to reduce technologically enhanced plagiarism must themselves become experts in conducting Internet searches and must learn about plagiarism-detection tools (Ercegovac & Richardson, 2004).

The increase in incidents of plagiarism by Net Generation students can be partly explained by their experience in using technology (Ercego-vac & Richardson, 2004). They grew up in a culture with fuzzy intellectual property ownership boundaries, including peer-to-peer file sharing, which essentially involves downloading copyrighted material (such as songs, games, and videos) without paying royalties to the copyright holders. Many Net Generation students engage in peer-to-peer file sharing and do not consider the ethical and legal implications. In the Net Generation Survey, 49% of students reported downloading music using file-sharing programs. In a course with first-year students, one of the authors (Junco) discusses intellectual property and cut-and-paste plagiarism at the start of the semester, with the assumption that his students have never been educated about these issues. It is clear to both authors that students come to college without appropriate knowledge about plagiarism and why it is unethical, and that they have trouble grasping the concepts even when they are explained. These students might think, "Why bother citing work when everything has always been mine for the taking on the Internet?" It is important for universities to engage in proactive activities throughout the curriculum and co-curriculum to help Net Gen students understand these important issues.

149

In addition to spawning new methods of plagiarism, technology has greatly influenced how Net Generation students write. While instant messaging keeps Net Gen students connected and helps them build interpersonal relationships (see chapter 3), it can have a deleterious effect on their writing skills. Data from the Net Generation Survey show that Net Gen students spend 80 minutes a day chatting via IM—much more time than they spend studying (more than 62% of students study 7 hours or less a week; Pryor, Hurtado, Saenz, Lindholm, Korn, & Mahoney, 2005). This is true of high school students as well; by the time they get to college, students have spent very little time on academic (formal) writing and much more time on nonacademic (informal) writing. Net Gen students are prone to make grammatical errors by writing in the same ways they write when they e-mail or IM. It is common to read student papers that include abbreviations and slang.

While Net Gen college students are on the bleeding edge of technology, faculty and student affairs staff (who are typically from other generations) often lag behind in their use of technology. Almost all faculty members have access to the Internet; however, only 69.2% use e-mail to communicate with their students. In addition, studies at various universities show that faculty who use course shells rarely or never use online chat, a component of those shells, with their students (Gaede, Svinicki, Herndon, Decker, & Evans, 2003; Turbin, 2005; Warburton, Chen, & Bradburn, 2002).

Other differences exist between faculty members and Net Gen students in the use of technology. For example, according to research by Shuell and Farber (2001) and Warburton et al. (2002), students reported using e-mail to communicate with faculty more than faculty reported using e-mail to communicate with students. It is possible that faculty members lack knowledge about how to integrate technology into their courses. Because they did not grow up with the technology, they generally require more training to adapt to it, and this training is not readily available (Roach, 2000). Faculty members are expected to engage in other tasks—such as research, publishing, grant writing, and service—in addition to course preparation, leaving little time for online course development.

SUMMARY

It is important for institutions of higher education to understand the divide between the technology skills of faculty and those of their wired Net Gen students, and to provide faculty with professional development opportunities that will help them enhance their technology skills. Professional development for faculty should also focus on the latest research on how

Net Generation students process and communicate knowledge. These two types of professional development will help faculty understand their Net Generation students and enable them to adapt their teaching techniques to suit all types of learners.

RECOMMENDATIONS

To effectively teach Net Generation students, faculty require different skill sets than they needed to teach earlier generations. Because of the wired world in which they grew up, Net Generation students are less able to pay attention for long periods of time (Prensky, 2001); on the other hand, they are better able to enhance their learning experiences through experiential, hands-on learning. Net Generation students crave interaction with their peers and professors, and faculty members who integrate interaction (either in person or online) into their courses will see improvement in educational outcomes for Net Generation students. The following are recommendations for the classroom:

☞ Provide opportunities for Net Generation students to capitalize on their strengths in experiential learning. Net Gen students prefer to arrive at their own knowledge and they learn best by interacting; therefore, it is important to increase the use of teaching strategies and techniques that capitalize on these qualities.

☞ Take advantage of Net Generation students' ability to multitask by providing assignments that allow them to address a number of topics simultaneously. Allow multitasking in the classroom by using instantaneous response systems and by modeling appropriate uses of multitasking.

☞ Get to know the students. Learn about their backgrounds and engage them by personalizing the course material.

Conveying a sense of shared ownership of learning helps increase Net Generation students' motivation to learn.

☞ Net Generation students need help understanding issues of intellectual property and plagiarism. Review how to use and cite sources appropriately, and when it is necessary to do so.

☞ Focus on technology in the classroom only as a tool for meeting the ultimate goal of enhanced interaction. Converting lectures to PowerPoint slides does nothing to enhance the interactivity of the course. Keep in mind that Net Gen students have short attention spans because of their fast-paced world, and plan accordingly.

☞ Since Net Gen students will rarely use the library, teach them how to identify legitimate articles, research, and sources on the Internet.

REFERENCES

American College Health Association. (2006). National College Health Assessment Web Summary. Retrieved October 4, 2006, from http://www. acha.org/projects_programs/ncha_sampledata.cfm

Calvert, S. L., Rideout, V. J., Woolard, J. L., Barr, R. F., & Strouse, G. A. (2005). Age, ethnicity, and socioeconomic patters in early computer use. *American Behavioral Scientist, 48(*5), 590–607.

Center for Academic Integrity (CAI). (2005). CAI Assessment Project Report. Retrieved October 4, 2006, from http://www.academicintegrity.org/ cai_research.asp

Chickering, A. W., & Gamson, Z. F. (1987). Seven principles for good practice in undergraduate education. *AAHE Bulletin, 39*(7), 3–7.

Epley, N., & Kruger, J. (2004). When what you type isn't what they read: The perseverance of stereotypes and expectancies over e-mail. *Journal of Experimental Social Psychology, 41,* 414–422.

Ercegovac, Z., & Richardson, J. V. (2004). Academic dishonesty, plagiarism included, in the digital age: A literature review. *College and Research Libraries, 65*(4), 301–319.

Gaede, C. S., Svinicki, M. D., Herndon, S. W., Decker, M. L., & Evans, S. W. (2003). Assessment and evaluation of the use of technology in teaching and learning at the University of Texas at Austin: Final report for 2002–2003. Division of Instructional Innovation and Assessment, University of Texas at Austin. Retrieved October 4, 2006, from http://www.utexas. edu/academic/diia/research/measurement/iac/iac-factech-report.pdf

Hartman, J., Moskal, P., & Dziuban, C. (2006). Preparing the academy of today for the learner of tomorrow. In D. G. Oblinger & J. L. Oblinger (Eds.), *Educating the Net Generation*. Washington, DC: EDUCAUSE.

Jones, S. (2002). *The Internet goes to college: How students are living in*

153

the future with today's technology. Washington, DC: Pew Internet and American Life Project.

Junco, R. (2005). Technology and today's first-year students. In M. L. Upcraft, J. N. Gardner, B. O. Barefoot, & associates (Eds.), *Meeting challenges and building support: Creating a climate for first-year student success* (pp. 221–238). San Francisco: Jossey-Bass.

Junco, R., & Mastrodicasa, J. (2006). How to meet millennials' expectations (part 2). *NetResults.* Accessible at www.naspa.org/membership/mem/nr/article.cfm?id=1535

Kaiser Family Foundation. (2005). Generation M: Media in the lives of 8–18-year-olds. Retrieved October 4, 2006, from http://www.kff.org/entmedia/7251.cfm

Kruger, J., Epley, N., Parker, J., & Ng, Z-W. (2005). Egocentrism over e-mail: Can we communicate as well as we think? *Journal of Personality and Social Psychology, 89*(6), 925–936.

Kuh, G. D. (2003). What we're learning about student engagement from NSSE. *Change, 35*(2), 24–32.

Langlais, P. J. (2006, January 13). Ethics for the next generation. *Chronicle of Higher Education,* B11.

Lipka, S. (2005, December 16). State legislators as co-pilots. *Chronicle of Higher Education,* A22–A23.

Long, H. E., & Coldren, J. T. (2006, Spring). Interpersonal influences in large lecture-based classes: A socioinstructional perspective. *College Teaching, 54*(2), 237–243.

Lowery, J. W. (2004). Student affairs for a new generation. In M. D. Coomes & R. DeBard (Eds.), *Serving the millennial generation: New directions for student services, no. 106* (pp. 87–99). San Francisco: Jossey-Bass.

McNeely, B. (2006). Using technology as a learning tool, not just the cool new thing. In D. G. Oblinger & J. L. Oblinger (Eds.), *Educating the Net Generation*. Washington, DC: EDUCAUSE.

Nelson Laird, T. F. & Kuh, G. D. (2005). Student experiences with information technology and their relationship to other aspects of student engagement. *Research in Higher Education, 46*(2), 211–233.

Oblinger, D. G., & Oblinger, J. L. (2006). Is it age or IT? First steps toward understanding the Net Generation. In D. G. Oblinger & J. L. Oblinger (Eds.), *Educating the Net Generation*. Washington, DC: EDUCAUSE.

Prensky, M. (2001). Digital narratives, digital immigrants (part 2): Do they really think differently? *On the Horizon, 9*(6), 1–6.

Pryor, J. H., Hurtado, S., Saenz, V. B., Lindholm, J. A., Korn, W. S., & Mahoney, K. M. (2005). *The American freshman: National norms for fall 2005*. Los Angeles, CA: Cooperative Institutional Research Program: Higher Education Research Institute, University of California, Los Angeles.

Ramaley, J., & Zia, L. (2006). The real versus the possible: Closing the gaps in engagement and learning. In D. G. Oblinger & J. L. Oblinger (Eds.), *Educating the Net Generation*. Washington, DC: EDUCAUSE.

Roach, R. (2000). Mastering technology's tools and techniques. *Black Issues in Higher Education, 17*(20), 28–31.

Roberts, G. (2006). Technology and learning expectations of the Net Generation. In D. G. Oblinger & J. L. Oblinger (Eds.), *Educating the Net Generation*. Washington, DC: EDUCAUSE.

Strauss, W., & Howe, N. (2006). *Millennials and the pop culture: Strategies for a new generation of consumers in music, movies, television, the Internet, and video games*. Great Falls, VA: LifeCourse Associates.

Shuell, T. J., & Farber, S. L. (2001). Students' perceptions of technology use in college courses. *Journal of Educational Computing Research, 24*(2), 119–138.

155

Turbin, M. S. (2005). Brief report of faculty survey of instructional technology use. Office of the Vice Provost for Academic and Campus Technology, University of Colorado at Boulder. Retrieved October 4, 2006, from http://www.colorado.edu/vpact/itsp/data/faculty2005.htm

Warburton, E. C., Chen, X., & Bradburn, E. M. (2002). *Teaching with technology: Use of telecommunications technology by postsecondary instructional faculty and staff in fall 1998*. Washington, DC: U.S. Department of Education National Center for Education Statistics.

Wilson, M. E. (2004). Teaching, learning, and millennial students. In M. D. Coomes & R. DeBard (Eds.), *Serving the millennial generation: New directions for student services, no. 106* (pp. 59–71). San Francisco: Jossey-Bass.

Windham, C. (2006). The student's perspective. In D. G. Oblinger & J. L. Oblinger (Eds.), *Educating the Net Generation*. Washington, DC: EDUCAUSE.

Chapter 9

Summary and Recommendations for Practice

Today's college students do not act the same way that students from previous generations did when they were in college. At first glance, Net Generation students seem to be aloof, uninterested, and unconnected to the world around them. In actuality, these students are very interested in succeeding in college and in their careers. They are connected to their friends and the world through the use of information technology, much more so than any other generation in history. These college students require changes in higher education and in the ways administrators and faculty members communicate with them.

Consider the differences between Net Generation students and members of the Silent Generation, Boomers, and Generation X who comprise most of the higher education faculty and staff workforce. The Net Generation is the most diverse generation in U.S. history; the 2000 Census found that more than 31% of them are from non-White families, and this percentage is growing. The latest figures released by the U.S. Census (2006) show that Latinos are in the majority in New Jersey and are approaching the majority in California and Texas, while African Americans have been in the majority in the District of Columbia for quite some time. Population changes have allowed members of the Net Generation to have more exposure than any previous generation to people from various ethnic and racial backgrounds, which has been shown to be an important first step in identity development and acceptance (Cross & Fhagen-Smith, 2001).

As explained throughout this book, Net Generation culture is very different from the cultures of the previous two generations: the Gen Xers and the Boomers. Young people in the Net Generation have rebelled against certain aspects of the previous two generations and have formed a unique peer personality. Strauss and Howe (2006) describe this process:

☞ First, each rising generation *breaks with the styles and attitudes* of the young adult generation, which no longer functions well in the new era.

☞ Second, each rising generation *corrects for what it perceives as the excesses* of the current midlife generation—parents and leaders—sometimes as a protest, other times with the implicit support of parents and leaders who seek to correct the deficiencies of the adult world.

☞ Third, each rising generation *fills the social role* being vacated by the departing elder generation, a role that now feels fresh, functional, desirable, even necessary for a society's well-being. Through the living memory of everyone else, this dying generation has filled a social role so firmly

as to prevent others from claiming it. Now, with its passing,
the role is available again to the young (pp. 47–48).

Thus, the Net Generation will "rebel against Gen-X styles and attitudes, correct for Boomer excesses, and fill the role vacated by the [Silent
Generation]" (Strauss & Howe, 2006, p. 48). Therefore, we can expect that
members of the Net Generation will be team players, unlike Generation
Xers, and that they will use technology for community, not individual, gain.

As we have described in this book, members of the Net Generation
have done just that—they are avid users of technology for social benefit.
They are frequent users of instant messaging, cell phones, blogs, and
social networking sites to stay in touch with each other and make new
friends. Their culture includes the qualities of being special, sheltered,
confident, conventional, team-oriented, achieving, and pressured. To those
from other generations, some of these qualities may seem like weakness-
es. However, these students also have the potential to be the next "great"
generation in U.S. history (Strauss & Howe, 2006).

Faculty and student affairs professionals have encountered unique
challenges in working with students from the Net Generation, not least the
fact that these students adopt and adapt to new technologies at a lightning
pace. A good example is a change that occurred with Facebook during the
time this book was being written. Facebook added a feature called a "news
feed" that automatically announced to each user's friends everything the
user did on the site: If the user added a new friend, all the user's friends
knew about it; if the user wrote on a friend's wall, all the user's friends
would be alerted to what was written. This feature (which some called "the
creepy stalker feature") caused a great deal of protest in the first few days
of its appearance. Students against the news feeds organized and protested
with an efficiency that is rarely seen in the non-virtual world. One student
newspaper reported on the events in real time:

[3:19 a.m. EST, Weds.] More than 100,000 Facebook users are members of an online petition within the site's groups feature. "Students Against Facebook News Feed" hit the 100,000 member mark at 2:11 a.m., Wednesday.

[12:22 p.m. EST, Weds.] In what is being described online as the first large-scale student protest since the 1960s, the "Students Against Facebook News Feed" membership continues to climb toward 200,000 members. At this time, there are more than 184,000 people attached to the group.

[1:11 p.m. EST, Weds.] More than 200,000 have joined the "Students Against Facebook News Feed."

[6:22 p.m. EST, Weds.] In four hours, the total membership for Facebook's News Feed protest group increased by 100,000. As of, 5:13 p.m. EST, the count sat at 300,033.

[8:17 p.m. EST, Weds.] Members continue to join the largest Facebook protest group, totalling [sic] 379,096 as of 8:15 p.m. EST. ...

[9:24 p.m. EST, Weds.] Just after 9 p.m. EST, membership for the "Students Against Facebook News Feed" group surpassed 400,000.

[10:13 p.m. EST, Thursday] The "Students Against Facebook News Feed" protest group crossed the 700,000 member mark at 9:37 p.m. Thursday. (Mazzola, 2006)

The protests about the news feeds were so immediate, powerful, and well organized that the Facebook developers quickly reworked the system and issued a statement explaining how users could "opt into" the news feed. The power of the Net Generation to use technology to organize so quickly and vigorously is a fitting metaphor for their generation—connected via technology, confident, team-oriented, and with the feeling that they are special and that they can change the world. Indeed, student affairs professionals can help to harness the positive qualities and energies of their Net Generation students for the common good.

Student affairs professionals must also change the ways in which they provide services for students. The Net Generation has been sheltered and protected by parents; these students and their parents expect institutions to provide safety services that are more rigorous and advanced than in the past. The increasing number of students with disabilities and mental health issues has caused institutions to rethink staffing in the areas of counseling and disability services. The tendency of these students' parents to be intensely involved in their children's lives has forced student affairs professionals to come up with ways to meet the needs of parents and, at the same time, keep them from disrupting the functions of student affairs divisions. Net Generation students' technological abilities and their insistence on fast communications have shaped student affairs communication policies and pressed student affairs professionals to work efficiently and effectively with e-mail and the Internet.

161

The Net Generation's values have also caused changes in the traditional workplace. Some of this generation's characteristics have led to new issues in career planning. For example, they may accept employment offers and then decline them when they receive better offers from different employers. Net Generation employees do well working in groups. They expect that they will work hard because they know they need to in order to reach their long-term goals. They expect their supervisors to be fair and to "follow the rules." There has been a shift in the workplace as more employees telecommute and Net Generation employees are comfortable with working "through" the Internet (Margulius, 2006). Net Generation students' parents have been involved in their transition to the world of work in much the same way that they are involved in their students' college careers. For example, a corporate recruiter told one of the authors (Junco) about how an applicant brought his mother to a job interview. When the applicant wasn't given the position, his mother called to try to change the employer's mind.

Academic advisors to the Net Generation have seen a shift in the values of their advisees. Advisors have found that they often need to be more direct with Net Gen students to help them articulate their goals, which are often vague. Net Gen advisees may continue to operate under the same model that helped them get into college—they act as if they were putting together a portfolio, and they are convinced that their short-term successes and planning are directly tied to the achievement of their long-term goals (Strauss & Howe, 2006). Advisors who have been accustomed to face-to-face appointments throughout their careers have seen significant increases in electronic communication, and some use technology that reaches the Net Generation in ways that are congruent with their tech-savvy mindsets. For example, the Division of Undergraduate Studies at The Pennsylvania State University has used podcasts to inform students, before they arrive on campus, about how the advising process works.

162

Faculty members face a number of challenges in working with the Net Generation in the classroom. Net Gen students process information differently than students from previous generations. Their ability to multitask is unparalleled; they often chat with multiple friends online while doing their schoolwork. Their attention spans are shorter, and they skip from topic to topic while multitasking, resulting in a "hypertext" cognitive style (Prensky, 2001). Faculty must learn new technologies to use in the classroom (such as SmartBoards and instant-response devices) if they want to keep the Net Generation engaged.

For the most part, the technologies that Net Generation students use are helpful to their psychosocial development as they reach out to others